Celebrate Colorado

West of the Rockies

Recipes for All Seasons

Junior Service League
of Grand Junction

Celebrate Colorado
West of the Rockies

Copyright © 2005

Junior Service League of Grand Junction

425 North Avenue, Suite B

Grand Junction, Colorado 81501

970-243-7790

www.jslgj.com

This cookbook is a collection of favorite recipes, which are not necessarily original recipes.

Nutritional Analysis: Pat Stiles

Photography © Christopher Tomlinson

Library of Congress Number: 2005920296

ISBN 0-9641314-1-2

Edited, Designed, and Manufactured by

Favorite Recipes Press

an imprint of

FRP

P.O. Box 305142

Nashville, Tennessee 37230

800-358-0560

Art Director: Steve Newman

Book Designer: Brad Whitfield, Susan Breining

Project Manager: Susan Larson

We gratefully acknowledge the information from *A Spirit of Charity 1896-1996,* Dave Fishell, 1996 and *A Land Alone: Colorado's Western Slope,* Duane Vandenbusche and Duane Smith, 1981

Manufactured in the United States of America

First Printing 2005

12,500 copies

June 1, 2005

Greetings from Grand Junction, Colorado!

As Mayor of Grand Junction, I am honored and pleased to endorse *Celebrate Colorado, West of the Rockies.* In the fine tradition of the Junior Service League of Grand Junction, this group once again has created a regional book worthy of nationwide recognition. Their previous cookbook, *West of the Rockies, Recipes from Campfire to Candlelight,* continues to be a favorite, having received national recognition during the past ten years.

Celebrate Colorado, West of the Rockies reflects the colorful tastes, cultures, and lifestyles of Western Colorado and the state of Colorado. Its creation reflects a community that values and promotes the spirit of voluntarism. The activities and work of the Junior Service League help make our community what it is today through contributions of time and money to worthy nonprofits. These contributions strengthen and enrich life in Western Colorado and help make our community a better place.

Yours truly,

Bruce Hill
Mayor

Dedication

These two pages are a dedication to cooks everywhere, and especially for the ones who have had a part in making me a decent cook.

When I was a child, my grandmother, Argie Cozza, taught me all the things a woman should know about cooking (especially for Italian men who, by the way, are very vocal about food). She was all the inspiration a young cook could ask for.

Being an Italian man, my father, Dick Cozza, taught me not to get offended when given "constructive criticism" about what I have cooked.

My mom, Joan Cozza, was the one who let me cook and cook and cook in her (very clean) kitchen as a child and into my teens. She never once got angry about the mess and always said nice things about the wild dishes I made her endure.

My dear friend Frances Holmes made every meal an event of monumental proportions and showed that being CRAZY to cook is not a character flaw.

My mother-in-law, Jean Francis, is, simply put, a good person with good sense and unbelievable patience. Those two qualities are a must for any good cook.

The one person who has really exercised acceptance for my near obsession with the kitchen is my daughter, Hannah Martinez. She is a great little spirit and gives meaning to all that is good in my world. She has endured hearing, "We will do it when I'm done in the kitchen" more than she should have had to. Thanks, Hannah, and I always try to remember not everyone loves to cook.

My life is the best because of my husband, Mark Francis. Mark built me the ultimate dream kitchen, where for so many hours I have enjoyed life with my stove. You are right, "If I could dream it, you could build it." Boy, have you ever! I love you.

Love and Thanks,
Jan Cozza-Francis

Best of luck to the Junior Service League in their fund-raising endeavors with this cookbook.

Preface

The sheer existence of all living things depends on food and drink. If you stop and think of it, nearly every event has a culinary element that makes it unique in and of itself. Whether it be a hot dog at a ball game, a turkey at Christmas, or the sweet smell of barbecue on a summer's evening, our experiences are surrounded by food.

The following pages are filled with the memories of things enjoyed by the authors, the Junior Service League of Grand Junction. Its intention is to preserve the tradition of recording a variety of heartfelt dishes and drinks—all to be handed down as our grandmothers and their grandmothers did, thus preserving the moments captured in kitchens across the world.

Celebrate the effort, celebrate the times, and celebrate the uniqueness of this compilation of recipes.

Celebrate the Seasons of Colorado, West of the Rockies!

Underwritten by Jan Francis

Sponsor

Mark and Jan Francis

Contents

Foreword

I am honored to write the foreword for the Junior Service League of Grand Junction's new cookbook. As a food professional, I was most impressed with their first cookbook and am looking forward to the publishing of their latest culinary venture. They spent unlimited hours testing and developing recipes you can count on for accuracy and good taste. Creating a good cookbook is no easy undertaking, but it is typical of the energy, dedication, and time they are willing to put forth in all of their worthwhile community projects.

I had firsthand experience with JSL members when working with them for a couple of years on their Walk for Life Event, held in October of each year, to provide funds for free mammograms for underinsured and uninsured women in Mesa County. I saw firsthand the cooperation and immediate action of all members in taking on responsibilities to make their event the best it could be.

The commitment of JSL members has provided over $200,000 in grants and 10,000 hours of community service in five years! I congratulate the Junior Service League on the success of all their projects, including Walk for Life, Make a Difference Day, and Viva el Vino. JSL definitely helps to enhance the quality of life for so many in this community. I thank them and wish them good luck with this new cookbook that will enable them to continue their good work.

Dixie Burmeister

Icon Information ~ *From Anasazi Petroglyphs*

Indicates a Sponsor

Indicates the recipe was contributed
by a restaurant

Recipient List

Over the past fourteen years the Junior Service League of Grand Junction has given out over $443,000 to many worthy recipients in the community, including the following:

Art Heritage	Junior Service League Park
B4 Babies	Latimer House
Botanical Gardens	Marillac Clinic
CASA	Mesa County Health Department
Center for Independence	Mesa Developmental Services
Chipeta Girl Scouts	Mesa State College Foundation
Community Hospital	Partners
Dinosaur Valley Museum	Pro Bono Project
Effective Parents Project	Retired and Senior Volunteer Program
Girls on the Run	Riverfront Commission
Go EI Inc.	St. Mary's Hospital
Grand Valley Audubon	School District 51
Grand Valley Catholic Outreach	The Tree House
Habitat for Humanity	UTEC Scholarship
Hilltop's Choice Program	Western Colorado Center for the Arts
Hope Haven	Western Slope Center for Children
Hospice of the Grand Valley	

Introduction

We are privileged to live in the Grand Valley, where we are blessed to be able to celebrate four fabulous seasons. West of the Rocky Mountains, in the high desert of the Grand Valley, we are surrounded by the breathtaking vistas of Grand Mesa, the Colorado Plateau, and the Bookcliffs. We have hundreds of lakes, rivers, and forests that are home to a bounty of wildlife and thousands of miles of trails for wandering in the wilderness.

The change of seasons brings a change of tastes to match the occasion. *Celebrate Colorado* is a collection of recipes, an extension of ourselves, including new recipes and those handed down through generations. What better way to bring neighbors, friends, and families together to explore the flavors of our region? Each recipe was carefully chosen, tested, and compiled to ensure a superb cookbook to be read, cherished, and handed down to the next generation.

As aspen leaves fall, apple cider simmering and peach pies cooling are signs of approaching autumn. Junior Service League members hit the ground running (well actually, walking) into one of our major fund-raising events. The Walk for Life raises money for breast-cancer detection and prevention in our community. Fall is also the time to explore the many roadside stands where the local farmers proudly display their abundant fresh vegetables and fruits. One of the oldest and most enjoyable of the festivals is the Fruita Fall Festival, where you can enjoy food, fun, and friends. Grand Mesa in the fall is ablaze with the changing foliage of brilliant gold and orange as the aspen trees pose for photographers on Color Sunday.

Winter is especially attractive when snow falls on Grand Mesa, and Powderhorn Ski Resort is open for business. It's a great time for breads fresh from the oven, homemade soups, and spirited beverages that always taste better when shared with friends and family. The holiday season is the perfect time to celebrate and share favorite recipes.

When spring arrives, the Grand Valley is dotted with the buds of beautiful, fragrant blossoms of fruit trees and grapevines. Another sure sign of spring—the Junior Service League's Viva el Vino event, a fund-raiser that brings the community out to enjoy good food, company, and the best wines of local vintners.

Summer is the season of abundant sun and visitors from all over the world here to enjoy the outdoors. Mountain biking, hiking, and fishing in the Colorado high country build a hearty appetite for fresh salsas, salads, and local wines. We celebrate the abundance at downtown Grand Junction's weekly Farmers Market. Summer fun is not complete without the enjoyment of live music, local hospitality, and the opportunity to sample the flavor of the famous locally grown crops.

We hope you enjoy our book. Many thanks go out to our families, friends, and community for sharing their recipes and support with us. It has been our pleasure to put this book together for you, and it will be an incredible joy for us to share the proceeds from this book with our community.

Sincerely,

Kathleen Copeland and Joan Graham
Junior Service League of Grand Junction

Spring

Breakfast, Breads & Appetizers

Spring Menu

Roast Leg of Lamb
page 86

Twice-Baked Potatoes
page 67

Spinach Baked with Feta
page 111

Champagne Vinaigrette
page 54

Citrus-Glazed Carrots
page 61

Quick Caramel Pecan Rolls
page 23

Lemon Curd Bars
page 138

Sponsored

Tubac Deli Quiche

1 (12-inch) flour tortilla
1 cup sliced mushrooms
1/2 cup diced celery
1/2 cup chopped green bell pepper
1/2 cup chopped onion
1 cup baby spinach leaves, julienned
2 tablespoons vegetable oil
8 ounces diced bacon, ham or
   sausage, cooked
5 eggs
1 1/2 cups half-and-half
1 teaspoon salt
1/4 teaspoon pepper
1 cup (4 ounces) shredded
   Cheddar cheese

Warm the tortilla on a hot grill or in a nonstick skillet over medium heat. Line the pie plate with the tortilla. Sauté the mushrooms, celery, bell pepper, onion and spinach in the oil in a skillet. Stir in the bacon. Spoon into the tortilla-lined pie plate. Whisk together the eggs, half-and-half, salt and pepper in a medium bowl. Pour over the vegetable mixture. Top with the cheese. Bake at 425 degrees for 15 minutes. Reduce the heat to 300 degrees and bake 30 minutes longer or until firm. Cool 5 minutes before cutting. Note: If using frozen chopped spinach, thaw and squeeze dry.

Mexican Variation: Add 1/2 cup salsa and 1/4 cup chopped green chiles to the egg mixture.

Makes 6 servings

From

Tubac Deli

Per serving
Calories 480 • Fat 40 g • Cholesterol 245 mg • Sodium 1040 mg • Carbohydrate 12 g • Fiber 2 g • Protein 18 g

Cheddar, Vegetable and Sausage Strata

*Around 1887 the first
Mesa County Fair was
held, and the first Peach
Days were held in
September 1891.*

—Mesa County Colorado:
A 100-Year History

Sponsored By

**JANICE BURTIS
HAMMOND**

Re/Max 4000, Inc.

2478 Patterson Road

Suite #1

Grand Junction, CO 81505

(970) 270-4444

9	(1-inch-thick) slices French bread (about 4 inches wide)
5	eggs
1	teaspoon basil
1	teaspoon Dijon mustard
1/2	teaspoon salt
1 1/2	cups half-and-half
	Pepper to taste
2	cups (8 ounces) shredded sharp Cheddar cheese
1/2	green bell pepper, julienned
15	cherry tomatoes, halved
6	ounces smoked sausage (such as kielbasa), cubed
2	tablespoons minced onion
	Chopped parsley

Arrange 8 of the bread slices in a buttered 9×13-inch baking dish. Cut remaining bread slice into 1-inch cubes and fit these into the spaces between the bread slices. Whisk together the eggs, basil, Dijon mustard and salt in a medium bowl. Whisk in the half-and-half. Pour the egg mixture over the bread. Refrigerate, covered, at least 2 hours or overnight. Sprinkle the strata with pepper. Top with half the cheese, then the bell pepper, tomatoes, sausage, onion and remaining cheese. Cover loosely with foil. Bake at 350 degrees for 20 minutes. Remove the foil; bake about 20 minutes longer or until the strata is set and the top is springy to the touch. Cool for 5 minutes. Sprinkle with the parsley.

Makes 6 servings

Per serving
Calories 760 • Fat 33 g • Cholesterol 260 mg • Sodium 1760 mg • Carbohydrate 83 g • Fiber 5 g • Protein 33 g

Baked Zucchini Frittata

5 eggs

5 cups shredded zucchini

1 cup chopped onion

1 1/2 cups baking mix

1/4 cup vegetable oil

1 teaspoon garlic powder

1 teaspoon salt

1/2 teaspoon pepper

1 tablespoon chopped parsley
(optional)

3/4 cup grated Parmesan cheese

Whisk the eggs in a large bowl. Add the zucchini, onion, baking mix, oil, garlic powder, salt, pepper and parsley; mix well. Pour into a buttered 9×13-inch baking dish. Bake at 350 degrees for 30 minutes. Sprinkle the cheese evenly over the top. Bake for 10 minutes longer.

Makes 6 servings

Sponsored By

Razzmatazz

Per serving

Calories 330 • Fat 20 g • Cholesterol 180 mg • Sodium 950 mg • Carbohydrate 28 g • Fiber 3 g • Protein 12 g

Breakfast Pizza

In a few 1880s issues of the Grand Junction Daily News, *there are vague references to a county fairgrounds located north of town. . . .The exact location of the county's very first—official or not— fairgrounds remains unsolved. . . .And if the First Fruit Ridge locale was indeed the first fairgrounds, we do know it didn't remain the fairgrounds for long. By the late 1890s Mesa County Fair events were being advertised at a new location along 12th Street and Gunnison Avenue, the current Lincoln Park.*

—A Spirit of Charity
1896-1996

1	(8-count) can refrigerator crescent rolls
1	pound bulk pork sausage, cooked and crumbled
1	cup frozen hash brown potatoes
1	tablespoon (or more) diced green bell pepper
1	tablespoon (or more) diced red bell pepper
1	cup (4 ounces) shredded sharp Cheddar cheese
3	eggs
1/4	cup milk
1/2	teaspoon salt
1/2	teaspoon pepper
2	teaspoons (or more) grated Parmesan cheese

Unroll the dough and separate into 8 triangles. Place on a 12-inch pizza pan with the points toward the center. Press the dough together to form a crust, sealing perforations. Sprinkle the sausage evenly over the crust. Top with the potatoes and bell peppers. Sprinkle with the Cheddar cheese. Whisk together the eggs, milk, salt and pepper in a small bowl. Pour over the crust. Sprinkle with the Parmesan cheese. Bake at 375 degrees for 25 to 30 minutes or until heated through.

Makes 6 servings

Per serving
Calories 520 • Fat 35 g • Cholesterol 205 mg • Sodium 1150 mg • Carbohydrate 21 g • Fiber 0 g • Protein 27 g

Night Before Breakfast

9   eggs

3   cups milk

1 1/2 teaspoons mustard

1   teaspoon salt

1 1/2 pounds bulk pork sausage, cooked
      and crumbled

1 1/2 cups (6 ounces) shredded
      Cheddar cheese

3   slices bread, cut into 1/4-inch cubes

Whisk together the eggs, milk, mustard and salt in a large bowl. Add the sausage, cheese and bread cubes and mix well. Pour into a greased 2-quart casserole. Refrigerate, covered, overnight. Bake, uncovered, at 350 degrees for 1 hour.

Makes 8 servings

Per serving

Calories 470 • Fat 35 g • Cholesterol 325 mg • Sodium 1430 mg • Carbohydrate 11 g • Fiber < 1 g • Protein 27 g

Oat and Cornmeal Waffles

1 egg

2 2/3 cups buttermilk

1/3 cup butter, melted (or canola oil)

2/3 cup rolled oats

2/3 cup cornmeal

1/2 cup all-purpose flour

3 tablespoons sugar

1 1/4 teaspoons baking soda

1/4 teaspoon salt

Whisk together the egg, buttermilk and melted butter in a bowl. Stir together the oats, cornmeal, flour, sugar, baking soda and salt in a large bowl. Add the buttermilk mixture to the flour mixture and mix well. Ladle the batter onto a hot waffle iron. Cook 3 1/2 to 4 minutes or until brown. Serve with warm fruit if desired.

Makes 4 servings

Sponsored By

Stewart Title of Grand Junction

Per serving

Calories 470 • Fat 22 g • Cholesterol 105 mg • Sodium 1090 mg • Carbohydrate 55 g • Fiber 3 g • Protein 14 g

Pumpkin Pancakes with Spiced Cider Syrup

PUMPKIN PANCAKES

1	cup all-purpose flour
1	tablespoon sugar
2	teaspoons baking powder
1/2	teaspoon salt
1/2	teaspoon ground cinnamon
2	egg yolks
1	cup milk
1/2	cup canned pumpkin
2	tablespoons vegetable oil
2	egg whites
	Spiced Cider Syrup (below)

SPICED CIDER SYRUP

3/4	cup apple juice
1/2	cup packed brown sugar
1/2	cup light corn syrup
2	tablespoons butter
1/2	teaspoon lemon juice
1/8	teaspoon ground cinnamon
1/8	teaspoon ground nutmeg

For the pancakes, stir together the flour, sugar, baking powder, salt and cinnamon. Whisk together the egg yolks, milk, pumpkin and oil in a large bowl until well blended. Stir in the flour mixture. Beat the egg whites in a small mixing bowl until moist peaks form. Fold into the pumpkin mixture. Pour a small amount of the batter onto a hot lightly greased griddle. Cook until bubbles appear on the surface and the underside is golden brown. Turn the pancake and cook until the underside is golden brown. Remove from the griddle and keep warm. Repeat with the remaining batter. Serve warm with Spiced Cider Syrup.

For the syrup, combine the apple juice, brown sugar, corn syrup, butter, lemon juice, cinnamon and nutmeg in a small saucepan. Bring to a boil. Boil for 2 to 3 minutes. Reduce the heat and simmer, uncovered, for 25 minutes. Let stand for 30 minutes before serving.

Makes 12 pancakes/6 servings

Per serving
Calories 370 • Fat 11 g • Cholesterol 85 mg • Sodium 490 mg • Carbohydrate 64 g • Fiber 1 g • Protein 6 g

Buttermilk Pancakes

I	cup all-purpose flour
1/2	teaspoon baking soda
1/4	teaspoon salt
I	egg white
I	egg yolk
I	cup buttermilk
I	tablespoon margarine or butter, melted

Stir together the flour, baking soda and salt. Beat the egg white in a small mixing bowl until moist peaks form; set aside. Whisk together the egg yolk and buttermilk in a medium bowl until blended. Stir in the flour mixture. Add the melted margarine; mix well. Fold in the egg white. Pour a small amount of the batter onto a hot lightly greased griddle. Cook until bubbles appear on the surface and the underside is golden brown. Turn the pancake and cook until the underside is golden brown. Remove from the griddle and keep warm. Repeat with the remaining batter. Serve with maple syrup.

Makes 2 servings

Per serving

Calories 375 • Fat 11.5 g • Cholesterol 115 mg • Sodium 810 mg • Carbohydrate 53 g • Fiber 2 g • Protein 14 g

Quick Caramel Pecan Rolls

1 cup packed brown sugar

1/2 cup (1 stick) margarine or butter

2 tablespoons water

1 cup chopped pecans

2 (8-count) cans refrigerator crescent rolls

Combine the brown sugar, margarine and water in a small saucepan. Bring to a boil. Cook until the brown sugar is dissolved, stirring frequently. Reserve 2 teaspoons of the pecans. Add the remaining pecans to the margarine mixture. Sprinkle the reserved pecans onto the bottom of a greased 10-cup bundt pan. Unroll the dough and form into crescent rolls as the package directs. Place the rolls in the prepared pan. Pour the caramel sauce over the rolls. Bake at 350 degrees for 30 minutes. Cool in the pan for 5 minutes. Invert onto a serving plate and slice to serve.

Makes 8 (2-slice) servings

Per serving

Calories 330 • Fat 23 g • Cholesterol 0 mg • Sodium 200 mg • Carbohydrate 32 g • Fiber 1 g • Protein 3 g

Blueberry Coffee Cake

COFFEE CAKE

3	eggs
1 1/2	cups sour cream
1 1/2	teaspoons vanilla extract
1	teaspoon grated lemon zest
2 1/2	cups all-purpose flour
1 1/2	cups granulated sugar
3/4	teaspoon baking powder
1/2	teaspoon baking soda
1/4	teaspoon salt
3/4	cup (1 1/2 sticks) butter, at room temperature
2	cups blueberries (preferably fresh) Walnut Streusel Topping (below)
1/2	cup confectioners' sugar
1	tablespoon milk

WALNUT STREUSEL TOPPING

1/3	cup packed light brown sugar
1/4	cup all-purpose flour
1/2	teaspoon ground cinnamon
1/4	cup (1/2 stick) butter, at room temperature
3/4	cup chopped walnuts

For the coffee cake, whisk together the eggs, sour cream, vanilla and lemon zest in a bowl until well blended; set aside. Stir together the flour, granulated sugar, baking powder, baking soda and salt in a large mixing bowl. Beat in the butter at low speed until smooth. Add the egg mixture and mix well. Pour 2/3 of the batter into a 9×13-inch baking pan coated with nonstick cooking spray. Sprinkle the blueberries evenly over the batter. Spread the remaining batter over the top, covering the blueberries. Sprinkle with the Walnut Streusel Topping. Bake at 350 degrees for 25 to 35 minutes or until a wooden pick inserted near the center comes out clean. Combine the confectioners' sugar and milk in a small bowl and mix until smooth. Drizzle over the coffee cake. Cool for 10 minutes before cutting.

For the topping, mix the brown sugar, flour and cinnamon in a bowl. Cut in the butter until crumbly. Add the walnuts and mix well.

Makes 12 servings

Per serving

Calories 500 • Fat 24 g • Cholesterol 105 mg • Sodium 190 mg • Carbohydrate 65 g • Fiber 2 g • Protein 7 g

Raspberry Streusel Coffee Cake

COFFEE CAKE

1	cup water
3 1/2	cups raspberries (unsweetened)
2	tablespoons lemon juice
1 1/4	cups granulated sugar
1/3	cup cornstarch
3	cups all-purpose flour
1	cup granulated sugar
1	teaspoon baking powder
1	teaspoon baking soda
1	cup (2 sticks) cold butter
2	eggs, lightly beaten
1	cup sour cream
1	teaspoon vanilla extract
	Streusel Topping (below)
1/2	cup confectioners' sugar
2	teaspoons milk
1/2	teaspoon vanilla extract

STREUSEL TOPPING

1/2	cup all-purpose flour
1/2	cup sugar
1/4	cup (1/2 stick) butter, softened
1/2	cup chopped pecans

For the coffee cake, combine the water and raspberries in a large saucepan. Cook over medium heat for 5 minutes. Add the lemon juice. Combine 1 1/4 cups granulated sugar and the cornstarch; stir into the raspberry mixture. Bring to a boil; cook for 2 minutes or until thickened, stirring constantly. Set aside to cool. Stir together the flour, 1 cup granulated sugar, baking powder and baking soda in a large bowl. Cut in the butter until crumbly. Stir in the eggs, sour cream and 1 teaspoon vanilla (the batter will be stiff). Spread half the batter in a greased 9×13-inch baking dish. Spread the raspberry filling over the batter. Spoon the remaining batter over the filling. Sprinkle with the Streusel Topping. Bake at 350 degrees for 40 to 45 minutes or until golden brown. Combine the confectioners' sugar, milk and 1/2 teaspoon vanilla in a small bowl and mix until smooth. Drizzle over the warm coffee cake. Cool for 10 minutes before cutting.

For the topping, combine the flour, sugar, butter and pecans in a small bowl and mix well.

Makes 16 servings

The Grand Junction Fruit Growers Association was formed in 1891 to market Grand Valley Fruit.

—Mesa County Colorado: A 100-Year History

Per serving
Calories 470 • Fat 21 g • Cholesterol 75 mg • Sodium 230 mg • Carbohydrate 66 g • Fiber 3 g • Protein 5 g

Toffee Banana Muffins

2 cups all-purpose flour

2 teaspoons baking powder

1 teaspoon baking soda

1/2 teaspoon salt

1/2 cup (1 stick) butter, at room temperature

1 cup sugar

2 eggs

1 cup mashed ripe bananas (about 2)

1/4 cup sour cream

1 teaspoon vanilla extract

1 cup crushed Enstrom's Almond Toffee

Stir together the flour, baking powder, baking soda and salt in a medium bowl and mix well. Cream the butter and sugar in a large mixing for bowl 3 minutes or until light and fluffy. Beat in the eggs 1 at a time. Add the bananas, sour cream and vanilla; mix well. Add the flour mixture, stirring just until combined (do not overmix). Fold in the crushed toffee. Coat 12 muffin cups with nonstick cooking spray or line with paper cups. Spoon the batter into the prepared pan, smoothing the batter on top. Bake at 350 degrees for 25 to 30 minutes or until a wooden pick inserted near the center comes out clean.

Makes 12 muffins

From

Enstrom's Candies

Per serving

Calories 280 • Fat 14 g • Cholesterol 65 mg • Sodium 360 mg • Carbohydrate 36 g • Fiber 1 g • Protein 4 g

Banana Nut Scones

3 cups all-purpose flour

1/2 cup packed brown sugar

2 teaspoons baking powder

1/2 teaspoon salt

1/4 teaspoon baking soda

3 tablespoons cold butter or margarine

2 egg whites

1/4 cup buttermilk

1 teaspoon vanilla extract

1 cup mashed ripe bananas (about 2)

1/3 cup coarsely chopped walnuts

1 tablespoon brown sugar

Stir together the flour, 1/2 cup brown sugar, baking powder, salt and baking soda in a large bowl. Cut in the butter with a pastry blender or 2 knives until crumbly. Whisk together the egg whites, buttermilk and vanilla in a small bowl until well blended. Add the buttermilk mixture and the bananas to the flour mixture, stirring just until moist (the dough will be wet and sticky). Turn the dough onto a lightly floured surface and knead lightly 4 times. Pat the dough into a 9-inch circle on a baking sheet coated with nonstick cooking spray. Sprinkle the walnuts and 1 tablespoon brown sugar over the dough; press gently into the dough. Cut into 12 wedges, cutting into, but not through, the dough. Bake at 400 degrees for 20 minutes or until golden brown.

Makes 12 scones

Per serving

Calories 220 • Fat 6 g • Cholesterol 10 mg • Sodium 230 mg • Carbohydrate 38 g • Fiber 2 g • Protein 5 g

Wonderful Holiday Bread

2 cups (4 sticks) butter, softened

2 1/2 cups sugar

6 eggs

2 ounces lemon extract

4 cups all-purpose flour

1 1/2 teaspoons baking powder

4 cups chopped pecans

1 pound golden raisins

Cream the butter and sugar in a large mixing bowl until light and fluffy. Beat in the eggs 1 at a time. Add the lemon extract; mix well. Sift together the flour and baking powder. Reserve 1/2 cup of the flour mixture. Add the remaining flour mixture gradually to the butter mixture and beat until smooth. Toss the pecans and raisins with the reserved flour; fold into the batter. Spoon into a greased and floured 10-cup tube pan. Bake at 275 degrees for 2 1/2 hours or until the bread tests done. Cool in the pan for 10 minutes. Remove to a wire rack and cool completely. Note: Nine miniature loaf pans may be used instead of the tube pan. Bake for 1 1/2 hours.

Makes 9 servings

Per serving

Calories 1380 • Fat 85 g • Cholesterol 250 mg • Sodium 590 mg • Carbohydrate 143 g • Fiber 9 g • Protein 16 g

Italian Cheese Bread

1   large loaf Italian or French bread (about 4 inches wide)
2   cups diced fresh tomatoes, drained
1   cup (4 ounces) shredded mozzarella cheese
1   cup (4 ounces) shredded Cheddar cheese
1   small onion, finely chopped
1/4   cup chopped black olives
1/4   cup Italian salad dressing
1   tablespoon chopped fresh basil

Slice off the top 1 inch of the bread loaf; set aside. Hollow out the loaf, leaving a 1/2-inch shell. Tear the bread from the center of the loaf into pieces. Combine the bread pieces, tomatoes, mozzarella cheese, Cheddar cheese, onion, olives, salad dressing and basil in a bowl; mix well. Spoon the cheese mixture into the bread shell; replace the top. Wrap in foil. Bake at 350 degrees for 25 minutes or until the cheese is melted. Slice and serve warm. Serve with your favorite pasta.

Makes 15 servings

Grand Junction's Chamber of Commerce boasted that "Grand Junction is a metropolitan city in every sense of the word," blessed with an "agreeable climate," recreational opportunities, excellent transportation facilities, shopping facilities equal to Denver or Salt Lake City, and a modern educational system. "The churches, the clubs, and the many fraternal organizations all contribute toward a wholesome social life. . . .One can live very economically in Grand Junction."

—A Land Alone: Colorado's Western Slope

Per serving
Calories 160 • Fat 7 g • Cholesterol 15 mg • Sodium 360 mg • Carbohydrate 18 g • Fiber 1 g • Protein 6 g

Blue Cheese Toasts

1/4 cup (1 ounce) crumbled blue cheese

2 tablespoons butter,
at room temperature

12 (1/2-inch-thick) slices sourdough
bread baguette
Sugar (optional)

Combine the cheese and butter in a small bowl and mix well. Spread the mixture on the bread slices and sprinkle with sugar if desired. Place the bread slices on a broiler pan. Broil for 1 minute or until bubbly.

Makes 12 servings

Per serving
Calories 290 • Fat 5.5 g • Cholesterol 5 mg • Sodium 630 mg • Carbohydrate 50 g • Fiber 3 g • Protein 9 g

Parmesan Rounds

1 bunch green onions, sliced

3/4 cup mayonnaise

1 1/2 cups grated Parmesan cheese

50 slices French bread baguette
(1 to 2 loaves)

Combine the green onions, mayonnaise and cheese in a bowl; mix well. Spread the mixture on the bread slices; arrange on a large baking sheet. Bake at 400 degrees for 15 minutes or until hot and light brown. Serve immediately.

Makes 50 servings

Per serving
Calories 160 • Fat 4.5 g • Cholesterol 5 mg • Sodium 320 mg • Carbohydrate 25 g • Fiber 1 g • Protein 5 g

Veggie Pizza Squares

1 (8-count) can refrigerator crescent rolls
8 ounces cream cheese, softened
1/3 cup mayonnaise
1/4 cup sour cream
1 envelope ranch salad dressing mix
1/2 cup chopped broccoli
1/2 cup chopped carrots
1/2 cup chopped cauliflower
1/2 cup chopped green bell pepper
1/2 cup chopped green onions
1/2 cup chopped tomato
1/2 cup (2 ounces) shredded Cheddar cheese

Unroll the dough and place in a 9×13-inch baking pan, pressing the dough out to cover the bottom of the pan. Press perforations together. Bake at 350 degrees for 7 to 8 minutes or until golden brown. Combine the cream cheese, mayonnaise, sour cream and ranch dressing mix in a mixing bowl and beat well. Spread the cream cheese mixture over the crust. Toss the vegetables together in a bowl and spoon evenly over the cream cheese layer. Sprinkle with the Cheddar cheese. Cover with plastic wrap and press the vegetables into the cream cheese layer. Refrigerate for 2 hours. Cut into bars and serve.

Makes 24 servings

Sponsored By

Les and Lynn Cotton

Focus Productions

. . .another great agricultural section of Western Colorado, the Grand Valley. That fertile valley, still called Grand because the Colorado River which runs through it was named such prior to 1921, is long and narrow, stretching from Glenwood Springs in the east to Grand Junction in the west.

—A Land Alone: Colorado's Western Slope

Per serving
Calories 80 • Fat 8 g • Cholesterol 15 mg • Sodium 85 mg • Carbohydrate 2 g • Fiber 0 g • Protein 2 g

Bacon and Cheese Canapés

1 1/2 cups (6 ounces) shredded Cheddar cheese

1 cup mayonnaise

8 to 12 ounces bacon, crisp-cooked and crumbled

1 small onion, finely chopped

8 slices firm white bread, crusts removed

Combine the cheese, mayonnaise, bacon, and onion in a small bowl and mix well. Spread the cheese mixture on 4 slices of the bread. Top with the remaining bread slices to form sandwiches. Wrap tightly and freeze. When ready to serve, cut each sandwich into quarters and place on a baking sheet. Bake at 325 degrees for 10 minutes.

Makes 16 servings

Per serving

Calories 190 • Fat 16 g • Cholesterol 25 mg • Sodium 230 mg • Carbohydrate 7 g • Fiber 0 g • Protein 4 g

Cheesy Onion Roll-Ups

8 ounces cream cheese, softened

1 cup sour cream

1/2 cup (2 ounces) finely shredded Cheddar cheese

3/4 cup sliced green onions

2 tablespoons hot red pepper sauce

1 tablespoon lime juice

1 tablespoon minced jalapeño chile

12 flour tortillas (6 inches in diameter)

Combine the cream cheese, sour cream, cheese, green onions, hot sauce, lime juice and jalapeño in a bowl and mix well. Spread the cheese mixture on 1 side of each tortilla and roll up tightly. Wrap tightly in plastic wrap; refrigerate for 1 hour or longer. Slice into 1-inch-thick pieces. Serve with picante sauce.

Makes 72 roll-ups/12 servings

Per serving

Calories 35 • Fat 2.5 g • Cholesterol 5 mg • Sodium 60 mg • Carbohydrate 3 g • Fiber < 1 g • Protein 1 g

Bacon Date Roll-Ups

12   slices bacon (1 pound)

24   blanched whole almonds
     (about 1/4 pound)

24   whole pitted dates (6 ounces)

Cut the bacon slices in half. Place an almond in each date. Wrap a piece of bacon around each stuffed date; secure with a toothpick. Place the roll-ups on a baking sheet. Bake at 400 degrees for 20 minutes.

Makes 24 servings

Per serving

Calories 140 • Fat 11 g • Cholesterol 15 mg • Sodium 160 mg • Carbohydrate 7 g • Fiber 1 g • Protein 3 g

Open-Face Crab Sammys

1   large loaf French bread
     (about 4 inches wide)

1/2   cup (1 stick) butter, softened

16   ounces cream cheese, softened

1   pound crab meat, drained and flaked

1/4   cup milk

1/2   (8-ounce) box Chick-n-a-Biscuit
     snack crackers, crushed

2   teaspoons Mrs. Dash seasoning

1   teaspoon garlic salt
     Paprika

Cut the bread into 1-inch thick slices. Spread the butter on 1 side of each bread slice. Place the bread slices on a baking sheet. Bake until brown and crisp. Combine the cream cheese, crab meat, milk, crushed crackers, seasoning and garlic salt in a medium bowl and mix well. Spread the crab mixture on the toasted bread slices. Sprinkle with the paprika. Bake at 350 degrees until lightly browned on top. Serve warm or chilled.

Makes 12 servings

Per serving

Calories 470 • Fat 25 g • Cholesterol 95 mg • Sodium 910 mg • Carbohydrate 42 g • Fiber 2 g • Protein 20 g

Maryland Crab Cakes

When Crawford learned that one of the last large tracts of unsettled land in the Rocky Mountains was going to be opened to ranchers, miners, homesteaders, and town builders such as himself, he jumped into action. When Crawford and other officers of his town company arrived at the junction of the Grand and the Gunnison rivers in late September 1881, he quickly laid out a town site about one mile square. . . .The founder was firm in his decision to call the new town Grand Junction.

—A Spirit of Charity
1896-1996

1/2 cup dry bread crumbs, or 6 saltines, crumbled
1/2 teaspoon dry mustard
1/2 teaspoon (or more) Old Bay seafood seasoning
1/8 teaspoon thyme
1/8 teaspoon oregano
1/4 teaspoon parsley flakes, or
1 teaspoon chopped fresh parsley
1 egg
1/2 cup mayonnaise
1/4 cup diced green or red bell pepper
1/2 teaspoon lemon juice
1/2 teaspoon Worcestershire sauce
1 pound crab meat, drained and flaked (back-fin crab meat if available)

Stir together the bread crumbs, dry mustard, seafood seasoning, thyme, oregano and parsley in a bowl. Whisk together the egg, mayonnaise, bell pepper, lemon juice and Worcestershire sauce in a large bowl; fold in the crumb mixture. Stir in the crab meat. Form into 12 cakes. Refrigerate for 2 hours or longer (to keep the cakes from breaking apart during cooking). Place the crab cakes on a broiler pan. Broil for 5 minutes on each side or until brown. Or, pan-fry in hot oil until brown; drain on paper towels before serving. Serve with tartar sauce if desired. Note: If there isn't time to refrigerate, form the crab mixture into balls and roll in cornflake crumbs. Broil until brown.

Makes 6 servings/2 crab cakes each

Per serving
Calories 260 • Fat 18 g • Cholesterol 105 mg • Sodium 510 mg • Carbohydrate 7 g • Fiber 0 g • Protein 19 g

Oysters Rockefeller

OYSTERS

Rock salt

12   oysters on the half shell

12   tablespoons Rockefeller Sauce (below)

1/4   cup freshly grated Parmesan cheese

ROCKEFELLER SAUCE

1   rib celery

1   yellow onion

1/4   bunch fresh parsley

3/4   bunch fresh spinach

1/2   cup (1 stick) butter

1/2   teaspoon salt

1/4   teaspoon pepper

1 1/2   teaspoons thyme

1/8   teaspoon Tabasco sauce

1/2   teaspoon Worcestershire sauce

1/3   cup bread crumbs

For the oysters, preheat the oven to 450 degrees. Fill two 9-inch pie plates with rock salt. Cut the oyster meat away from the shells. Rinse with cold water. Arrange 6 oysters in shells in the salt in each pie plate. Spoon 1 tablespoon Rockefeller Sauce over each oyster and sprinkle with Parmesan cheese. Bake for 10 to 20 minutes or until the cheese begins to brown. Serve immediately.

For the sauce, process the celery, onion, parsley and spinach in a food processor until finely chopped. Melt 1/4 cup of the butter in a saucepan over low heat. Add the chopped vegetables, salt and pepper. Simmer, covered, for 1 hour. Add the thyme, Tabasco sauce and Worcestershire sauce and mix well. Cook for 5 minutes. Add the bread crumbs and remaining 1/4 cup butter, stirring until the butter is melted. You may freeze any leftover sauce for another use.

Makes 4 servings

Per serving

Calories 430 • Fat 29 g • Cholesterol 140 mg • Sodium 820 mg • Carbohydrate 21 g • Fiber 3 g • Protein 20 g

Hot Ginger Wings

1 cup soy sauce

1/2 cup dry red wine

11/2 cups plus 1 tablespoon sugar

1/4 teaspoon (or more) ground ginger

Hot red pepper sauce to taste

4 pounds chicken wing drumettes

Combine the soy sauce, red wine, sugar, ginger and hot sauce in a small saucepan. Heat until the sugar dissolves. Place the chicken in a 9×13-inch baking pan. Pour the soy sauce mixture evenly over the chicken. Bake at 400 degrees for 45 minutes. Turn the chicken drumettes over and bake for 45 minutes longer.

Makes 8 servings of 6 to 8 wings

Walter Walker, William Moyer, Clyde Biggs, Ollie Bannister, and J. H. Rankin became the board of directors of the New Avalon Theater which opened in 1923. Shows included vaudeville, theater, and the new "talkies."

—Mesa County Colorado: A 100-Year History

Sponsored By

Jeff, Kathleen, and Averey Copeland

Per serving

Calories 590 • Fat 10 g • Cholesterol 235 mg • Sodium 3790 mg • Carbohydrate 53 g • Fiber 0 g • Protein 66 g

Artichoke Hearts with Lemon-Parmesan Sauce

ARTICHOKE HEARTS

3 (14-ounce) cans artichoke hearts, drained

Lemon-Parmesan Sauce (below)

2 1/2 cups (10 ounces) shredded whole milk mozzarella cheese

2/3 cup Italian-seasoned bread crumbs

1/2 cup pine nuts, toasted

LEMON-PARMESAN SAUCE

3/4 cup mayonnaise

1 3/4 cups evaporated milk

1 cup grated Parmesan cheese

Grated zest and juice of 1 large lemon

1 tablespoon chopped fresh parsley

1 tablespoon chopped fresh basil

2 teaspoons sugar

1/4 teaspoon coarsely ground pepper

For the artichokes, cut the artichoke hearts into halves lengthwise and arrange in a generously buttered 9×13-inch baking pan. Spoon the Lemon-Parmesan Sauce over the artichoke hearts. Sprinkle with the cheese and then the bread crumbs. Bake at 375 degrees for 25 minutes or until the cheese is bubbly around the edges of the pan. Remove from the oven. Sprinkle with the pine nuts and serve.

For the sauce, whisk together the mayonnaise, evaporated milk, cheese, lemon zest and juice, parsley, basil, sugar and pepper in a bowl until well blended. Refrigerate, covered, until ready to use. (May be made 3 days ahead.)

Makes 8 servings

From

Nero's Italian Restaurant

Per serving

Calories 490 • Fat 36 g • Cholesterol 65 mg • Sodium 1290 mg • Carbohydrate 23 g • Fiber 5 g • Protein 19 g

Onion Soufflé

1 (12- to 16-ounce) package frozen chopped onions

24 ounces cream cheese, softened

2 cups grated Parmesan cheese

1/2 cup mayonnaise

Thaw the onions; roll in paper towels to remove the excess moisture. Combine the onions, cream cheese, Parmesan cheese and mayonnaise in a large bowl and mix well. Spoon into a shallow 2-quart soufflé dish. Bake at 425 degrees for 15 minutes or until golden brown. Serve with corn chips or crackers. Note: The soufflé may be frozen before baking for later use.

Makes 12 servings

Sponsored By

Anne Connolly

Re/Max 4000, Inc.

Per serving

Calories 320 • Fat 29 g • Cholesterol 75 mg • Sodium 330 mg • Carbohydrate 5 g • Fiber 1 g • Protein 7 g

Rocky Mountain "Caviar"

2 tablespoons red wine vinegar

1 1/2 to 2 teaspoons Tabasco sauce

1 1/2 teaspoons vegetable oil

1 garlic clove, minced

1/8 teaspoon pepper

1 ripe avocado, cubed

1 (15-ounce) can black-eyed peas, drained and rinsed

1 (15-ounce) can whole kernel corn, drained and rinsed

2/3 cup thinly sliced green onions

2/3 cup chopped fresh cilantro

8 ounces Roma tomatoes, chopped

Salt to taste

Combine the vinegar, Tabasco sauce, oil, garlic and pepper in a large bowl and mix well. Add the avocado to the vinegar mixture and toss to coat. Add the black-eyed peas, corn, green onions, cilantro and tomatoes and mix well. Add salt to taste. Serve with chips. Note: Cabbage may be added to make a slaw. May also be served over baked potatoes.

Makes 16 (1/4-cup) servings

The event that really helped push Grand Junction forward took place in November 1882. Grand Junction found itself on the main line of the Denver & Rio Grande Western Railroad. The Rio Grande, and other rail systems that would link up to Grand Junction, all played an important part in turning the town into Western Colorado's largest business, medical, and population center.

—A Spirit of Charity
1896-1996

Per serving

Calories 70 • Fat 2.5 g • Cholesterol 0 mg • Sodium 160 mg • Carbohydrate 11 g • Fiber 3 g • Protein 2 g

Cranberry Cream Cheese Appetizer

16 ounces fresh cranberries

3/4 to 1 cup sugar

1/3 cup chopped cilantro

1 (4-ounce) can diced green chiles

2 green onions, chopped

8 ounces block-style cream cheese

Place the cranberries with enough water to cover in a saucepan. Bring to a boil. Cook until the berries start to pop. Drain the berries, reserving 1/4 cup of the liquid. Return the berries and the reserved liquid to the saucepan. Add the sugar, cilantro, green chiles and green onions and mix well. Refrigerate for 2 hours or until chilled. Place the cream cheese on a serving dish. Stir the cranberry mixture and pour over the cream cheese. Serve with assorted crackers.

Makes 32 servings

Per serving

Calories 430 • Fat 40 g • Cholesterol 120 mg • Sodium 370 mg • Carbohydrate 11 g • Fiber 1 g • Protein 8 g

Fantastic Fruit Dip

8 ounces cream cheese, softened

3/4 cup packed brown sugar

1/4 cup confectioners' sugar

3 tablespoons milk or half-and-half

1 teaspoon vanilla extract

Combine the cream cheese, brown sugar, confectioners' sugar, milk and vanilla in a mixing bowl and mix well. Serve with strawberries, apple slices or other fresh fruit.

Makes 16 servings

Per serving

Calories 100 • Fat 5 g • Cholesterol 15 mg • Sodium 50 mg • Carbohydrate 13 g • Fiber 0 g • Protein 1 g

Easy Cheesy "Fundue"

16   ounces cream cheese, softened
3/4   cup grated Parmesan cheese
1 1/2   cups milk
1/2   teaspoon garlic salt

Combine the cream cheese, Parmesan cheese, milk and garlic salt in a heavy saucepan. Heat over low heat for 10 to 15 minutes or until thickened, stirring constantly. (Use only low heat to avoid overcooking the cheeses.) Serve warm, fondue-style, with French or Italian bread cubes for dipping.

Makes 12 servings

Per serving
Calories 160 • Fat 14 g • Cholesterol 45 mg • Sodium 210 mg • Carbohydrate 3 g • Fiber 0 g • Protein 5 g

Antipasto Dip

1   (14-ounce) bottle ketchup
1   (12-ounce) jar cocktail sauce
1/4   cup creamy French salad dressing
2   (6-ounce) cans water-pack tuna, drained
8   ounces peeled cooked shrimp
     (may be fresh, or frozen and thawed)
1   (8-ounce) can sliced water chestnuts, drained
1   (5-ounce) jar green olives, drained and chopped
1   (5-ounce) jar cocktail onions, drained and chopped
1   (8-ounce) can white mushrooms

Combine the ketchup, cocktail sauce and French dressing in a large bowl and mix well. Add the tuna, shrimp, water chestnuts, olives, onions and mushrooms and stir gently. Refrigerate, covered, until chilled. Serve with crackers.

Makes 20 servings

Per serving
Calories 150 • Fat 4 g • Cholesterol 20 mg • Sodium 880 mg • Carbohydrate 20 g • Fiber 1 g • Protein 9 g

Peach Salsa

The first few months in Grand Junction were difficult. Many settlers spent the winter of 1881 in tents. Shelter had to be constructed, largely from cottonweeds growing along the river.

—Mesa County Colorado: A 100-Year History

10	medium peaches, peeled and chopped (2 1/2 to 3 pounds)
5	tomatoes, peeled and chopped
1	red onion, diced
1	red bell pepper, diced
3	large jalapeño chiles, seeded and minced
3	garlic cloves, crushed
1 1/2	tablespoons finely chopped fresh cilantro
2	tablespoons lime juice
2	tablespoons olive oil
1	tablespoon white vinegar
2	teaspoons Mexican seasoning
1/2	teaspoon (or more) salt
1/2	teaspoon cayenne pepper
1/2	teaspoon seasoned pepper

Combine the peaches, tomatoes, onion bell pepper, jalapeños, lime juice, olive oil and vinegar in a large stockpot and mix well. Season with the Mexican seasoning, salt, cayenne pepper and seasoned pepper. Bring to a boil; simmer for 5 minutes. Ladle the salsa into hot sterilized jars, leaving 1/2 inch headspace; seal with 2-piece lids. Process in a boiling water bath for 15 minutes. Serve with chips or use to accompany poultry, pork or burgers.

This recipe was a contest winner at the Palisade Peach Festival.

Makes 5 pints/20 (1/2-cup) servings

Per serving

Calories 45 • Fat 1.5 g • Cholesterol 0 mg • Sodium 115 mg • Carbohydrate 8 g • Fiber 1 g • Protein 1 g

Savory Shrimp and Artichoke Dip

1 (14-ounce) can artichoke hearts, drained
6 ounces frozen precooked peeled small shrimp
3 ounces cream cheese, softened
1/2 cup mayonnaise
1/2 cup salsa
1/3 cup grated Parmesan cheese
1 red bell pepper, diced
  Green onion tops, thinly sliced

Rinse and chop the artichoke hearts. Thaw the shrimp and squeeze dry in paper towels. Combine the artichoke hearts, shrimp, cream cheese, mayonnaise, salsa and Parmesan cheese in a large bowl and mix well. Spoon into a 9-inch pie plate or shallow baking dish. Bake at 350 degrees for 20 minutes. Top with the bell pepper and green onions. Serve with tortilla chips or assorted fresh vegetables.

Makes 16 servings

Sponsored By

Synthia and Leonard Polzine

Per serving

Calories 100 • Fat 8 g • Cholesterol 30 mg • Sodium 260 mg • Carbohydrate 4 g • Fiber 1 g • Protein 4 g

Green Lip Mussels in Champagne Cream Sauce

2   cups heavy cream

1   cup Champagne

1   cup white cooking wine

3   pounds green lip mussels, scrubbed, shucked if desired

     Capers to taste

Stir together the cream, Champagne and cooking wine in a bowl. Arrange the mussels in a shallow baking dish. Pour the cream mixture over the mussels. Sprinkle with the capers. Bake at 350 degrees for 20 minutes or until bubbly. Serve warm with toast rounds. Note: For an entrée, serve over angel hair pasta.

Makes 10 servings

Per serving

Calories 250 • Fat 20 g • Cholesterol 90 mg • Sodium 340 mg • Carbohydrate 8 g • Fiber 0 g • Protein 12 g

Tuna Tartare

8 to 16 ounces very cold sushi-quality tuna (yellow-fin or ahi)

1/2 cup olive oil

1/4 cup capers, chopped

1 to 2 green onions, chopped

2 teaspoons lemon juice

2 teaspoons Dijon mustard

1 teaspoon salt

1/2 teaspoon pepper

1/2 teaspoon dried chives, or 1 tablespoon fresh chives

Wasabi to taste (optional)

Cut the tuna into 1/8-inch cubes; refrigerate. Whisk together the olive oil, capers, green onions, lemon juice, Dijon mustard, salt, pepper, chives and wasabi until well blended. Fold the tuna into the olive oil mixture. Serve immediately with crackers. Note: Don't add tuna until all the dressing ingredients are mixed or the tuna will darken.

Makes 4 servings

Irrigation was essential and developed agriculture as well as drinking water. Since many did not boil their water, typhoid and dysentery were common, and "Belleyache Flats" became the town's nickname.

—Mesa County Colorado: A 100-Year History

Per serving
Calories 420 • Fat 34 g • Cholesterol 45 mg • Sodium 1010 mg • Carbohydrate 1 g • Fiber 0 g • Protein 27 g

Summer

Soups, Salads & Sides

Summer Menu

Watermelon Margaritas

page 148

Hot Ginger Wings

page 36

Double-Sauced Baby Back Ribs

page 92

Campfire Potatoes

page 65

Apple Baked Beans

page 59

Spinach and Romaine Salad

page 53

Peaches and Cream Cheese Bars

page 139

Mixed Greens with Spiced Pears and Almonds

1/4 teaspoon cayenne pepper

1/4 teaspoon ground coriander

1/4 teaspoon ground cumin

1/4 teaspoon salt

1 tablespoon canola oil

1 cup sliced almonds

1 tablespoon butter

3/4 teaspoon turmeric

2 teaspoons honey

2 large Bosc pears, peeled and diced

Pinch of salt

2 tablespoons balsamic vinegar

1 teaspoon honey

1/4 cup olive oil

Salt and pepper to taste

8 ounces mixed salad greens

4 ounces goat cheese, crumbled (1 cup)

Stir together the cayenne pepper, coriander, cumin and 1/4 teaspoon salt in a medium bowl. Heat the canola oil in a medium skillet and add the almonds. Cook over medium heat for 2 minutes or until golden brown, stirring constantly. Add the hot almonds to the spice mixture, stirring to coat. Spread the nuts on a plate or waxed paper to cool. Melt the butter in the same skillet. Add the turmeric after the foam subsides. Cook and stir over medium-high heat for 30 seconds or until fragrant. Stir in 2 teaspoons honey. Add the pears and a pinch of salt. Cook for about 3 minutes, turning over once. Remove the pears to a plate. Whisk the vinegar with 1 teaspoon honey in a small bowl. Whisk in the olive oil until blended. Season with salt and pepper. Combine the greens and goat cheese in a large serving bowl. Add the dressing and toss. Top with the almonds and pears and serve.

Makes 8 servings

Pears, apples, peaches, and cherries made up the great fruit orchards of the Grand Valley; they were responsible for the birth of both Palisade and Fruita, and aided greatly in the growth of Grand Junction.

—A Land Alone: Colorado's Western Slope

Per serving
Calories 260 • Fat 21 g • Cholesterol 20 mg • Sodium 60 mg • Carbohydrate 11 g • Fiber 3 g • Protein 7 g

Charlemagne Salad

1 head each curly endive, romaine and iceberg lettuce, torn
1/2 cup olive oil
4 teaspoons minced shallots
2 teaspoons minced garlic
1/2 cup sherry vinegar
2 tablespoons fresh lemon juice
2 tablespoons Dijon mustard
10 ounces Brie cheese, chopped
Salt and pepper to taste
1 1/2 cups garlic croutons

Place the endive, romaine and iceberg lettuce in a large serving bowl. Heat the olive oil in a large skillet over low heat for 10 minutes. Add the shallots and garlic; cook for 5 minutes, stirring constantly. Whisk in the vinegar, lemon juice and Dijon mustard. Add the cheese and heat over low heat until the cheese is melted, stirring constantly. Season with salt and pepper. Pour over the greens and toss. Stir in the croutons and serve.

Makes 12 servings

Per serving
Calories 300 • Fat 21 g • Cholesterol 25 mg • Sodium 560 mg • Carbohydrate 18 g • Fiber 2 g • Protein 12 g

Salad Greens with Pears, Nuts and Blue Cheese

5 ounces mixed baby greens
2 ripe pears, sliced thinly lengthwise
1/2 cup (2 ounces) crumbled blue cheese
1/2 cup coarsely chopped pecans, toasted
1/4 cup raspberry vinegar
1 tablespoon Dijon mustard
1 teaspoon sugar
1/2 cup plus 2 tablespoons light extra-virgin olive oil
Salt and pepper to taste

Combine the greens, pears, blue cheese and pecans in a large serving bowl. Whisk together the vinegar, Dijon mustard and sugar in a small bowl. Whisk in the olive oil gradually until blended. Season with salt and pepper. Pour the dressing over the salad and toss.

Makes 6 servings

Per serving
Calories 330 • Fat 33 g • Cholesterol 10 mg • Sodium 530 mg • Carbohydrate 7 g • Fiber 1 g • Protein 3 g

Cranberry and Feta Green Salad with Balsamic Vinaigrette

BALSAMIC VINAIGRETTE

2	tablespoons raspberry vinegar
1	tablespoon balsamic vinegar
1	tablespoon brown sugar
1	tablespoon chopped shallots
1/2	teaspoon honey Dijon mustard
1/4	cup vegetable oil
	Salt and pepper to taste

For the vinaigrette, whisk together the raspberry vinegar, balsamic vinegar, brown sugar, shallots and Dijon mustard in a small bowl. Whisk in the oil until blended. Season with salt and pepper.

SALAD

6	cups torn salad greens
	Balsamic Vinaigrette (above)
1/2	cup (2 ounces) crumbled feta cheese
1/2	cup dried cranberries

For the salad, place the greens in a large serving bowl. Pour the vinaigrette over the greens and toss. Stir in the cheese and cranberries. Note: Strawberry halves or mandarin oranges may be used instead of the cranberries.

Makes 4 servings

Sponsored By

Cheri Bahrke

Per serving

Calories 240 • Fat 16 g • Cholesterol 5 mg • Sodium 630 mg • Carbohydrate 24 g • Fiber 3 g • Protein 4 g

Toasted Almond Spinach Salad with Sesame Seed Dressing

SALAD

1	tablespoon butter
3/4	cup slivered almonds
16	ounces spinach, torn into bite-size pieces
1	cup dried cranberries
	Sesame Seed Dressing (below)

SESAME SEED DRESSING

1/4	cup cider vinegar
1/4	cup white wine vinegar
1/2	cup sugar
2	tablespoons sesame seeds, toasted
1	tablespoon poppy seeds
2	teaspoons minced onion
1/4	teaspoon paprika
1/2	cup vegetable oil

For the salad, melt the butter in a saucepan over medium heat. Add the almonds and cook until lightly toasted, stirring constantly. Cool. Combine the toasted almonds, spinach and cranberries in a large serving bowl. Pour the dressing over the salad and toss.

For the dressing, whisk together the cider vinegar, white wine vinegar, sugar, sesame seeds, poppy seeds, onion and paprika in a bowl. Whisk in the oil until blended.

Makes 8 servings

Sponsored By

Traeana Tripoli

Per serving

Calories 330 • Fat 22 g • Cholesterol 5 mg • Sodium 100 mg • Carbohydrate 35 g • Fiber 5 g • Protein 4 g

Spinach and Romaine Salad

DRESSING

1/4   cup lemon juice

2   egg yolks, or an equivalent amount of pasteurized egg substitute

1   garlic clove, minced

1/2   teaspoon salt

1/2   teaspoon pepper

1/2   teaspoon sugar

1/4   teaspoon dry mustard

2/3   cup vegetable oil

SALAD

8   ounces spinach, torn into bite-size pieces

1/2   head romaine, torn into bite-size pieces

8   ounces mushrooms, sliced

6   slices bacon, crisp-cooked and crumbled

3   green onions, chopped

For the dressing, combine the lemon juice, egg yolks, garlic, salt, pepper, sugar and dry mustard in a blender or food processor. Process for 2 minutes. Add the oil in a fine stream, processing constantly until smooth. Process for 2 minutes longer or until dressing thickens slightly. This can be prepared 2 hours in advance and refrigerated until ready to use.

For the salad, place the spinach, romaine, mushrooms, bacon and green onions in a large bowl and chill until serving time. Pour the dressing over the salad just before serving.

Makes 4 servings

The fast-running rivers of Western Colorado have increasingly attracted thrill-seekers to their waters. River-running with kayaks and rubber rafts has become a popular sport in the spring of the year when the rivers run full.

—A Land Alone: Colorado's Western Slope

Per serving

Calories 560• Fat 54 g • Cholesterol 125 mg • Sodium 680 mg • Carbohydrate 13 g • Fiber 4 g • Protein 9 g

Champagne Vinaigrette

1/3 cup Champagne vinegar

1/3 cup white wine

2 teaspoons Dijon mustard

1 tablespoon sugar, or to taste

1/3 cup corn oil or canola oil

Whisk together the vinegar, wine, Dijon mustard and sugar in a small glass bowl until the sugar is dissolved. Whisk in the corn oil until blended. Store, tightly covered, in the refrigerator for up to 2 weeks. Toss with your favorite green salad. Suggested salad combination: baby spinach or mixed salad greens, grapefruit sections, crumbled blue cheese, red onion slices, toasted pine nuts and avocado. Fresh herbs such as tarragon, parsley or basil may be added. Use other vinegars and seasonings, such as sherry vinegar; tarragon vinegar and capers; raspberry vinegar and chives.

Makes 4 servings

Per serving

Calories 200 • Fat 19 g • Cholesterol 0 mg • Sodium 65 mg • Carbohydrate 6 g • Fiber 0 g • Protein 0 g

Asian Slaw

2 cups finely shredded cabbage

1/3 cup chopped green onions

1 tablespoon slivered almonds

2 tablespoons rice vinegar

1 tablespoon sesame oil

1 teaspoon sugar

1/4 teaspoon crushed red pepper

Combine the cabbage, green onions and almonds in a bowl. Whisk together the vinegar, oil, sugar and red pepper in a small bowl until blended. Pour over the cabbage mixture and mix well.

Makes 2 servings

Per serving

Calories 120 • Fat 9 g • Cholesterol 0 mg • Sodium 15 mg • Carbohydrate 10 g • Fiber 3 g • Protein 2 g

Mushroom Bean Salad

MARINADE

1/2	cup wine vinegar
1	tablespoon sugar
1	small garlic clove, minced
1	teaspoon salt
1/2	teaspoon basil
1/2	teaspoon oregano
1/2	teaspoon white pepper
1/4	teaspoon dry mustard
2/3	cup vegetable oil

SALAD

1	(15-ounce) can garbanzo beans, drained and rinsed
1	(15-ounce) can green beans, drained and rinsed
1	(15-ounce) can kidney beans, drained and rinsed
1	garlic clove, minced
8	ounces mushrooms, sliced
1	onion, sliced into rings

For the marinade, whisk together the vinegar, sugar, garlic, salt, basil, oregano, pepper and dry mustard in a small bowl. Whisk in the oil until blended.

For the salad, combine the garbanzo beans, green beans, kidney beans, garlic, mushrooms and onion in a large bowl. Pour the marinade over the bean mixture and mix well. Marinate, covered, in the refrigerator for several hours to blend flavors. Serve chilled.

Makes 16 servings

The National Junior College Athletic Association World Series (JUCO) Tournament has been held in Grand Junction since 1959.

—Mesa County Colorado: A 100-Year History

Per serving

Calories 140 • Fat 10 g • Cholesterol 0 mg • Sodium 390 mg • Carbohydrate 10 g • Fiber 3 g • Protein 4 g

Sundance Salad

1	cup dried black beans
1	cup dried pinto beans
8	cups hot water
1	teaspoon salt
1	cup Newman's Own Balsamic Vinaigrette
1	cup Newman's Own Medium Salsa
2	cups finely chopped jicama
1	cup diced red onion
1	cup chopped green onions
1	red bell pepper, finely chopped
1/4	cup finely chopped pickled jalapeño chiles
1	garlic clove, minced
2	tablespoons finely chopped fresh cilantro
1/4	teaspoon Tabasco sauce
1/4	teaspoon coarsely ground pepper
	Lettuce

Sort and rinse the beans. (Keep the pinto beans and black beans separate until after cooking so that each kind retains its own color and flavor.) Soak the beans separately in water to cover in a saucepan overnight. (Or, for faster soaking, bring the beans to a boil separately in 4 cups water in a 2-quart saucepan. Let the beans stand, covered for 1 hour.) Drain the soaked beans and place in separate saucepans. Add 4 cups hot water and 1/2 teaspoon salt to each pan. Bring to a boil; reduce the heat and simmer, partially covered, for about 2 hours or until the beans are tender but not mushy. Drain. Place the warm or room-temperature beans in a large bowl and add the balsamic vinaigrette. Marinate, covered, in the refrigerator for 2 to 4 hours. Add the salsa, jicama, red onion, green onions, bell pepper, jalapeños, garlic, cilantro, Tabasco sauce and pepper and toss gently. Let stand for 2 to 4 hours or overnight to blend flavors. Serve on a bed of lettuce and garnish with sliced Roma tomatoes. Serve with tortilla chips or wheat crackers. Note: This salad keeps well in the refrigerator for several days.

Makes 15 (1/2 cup) servings

Per serving

Calories 120 • Fat 0 g • Cholesterol 0 mg • Sodium 380 mg • Carbohydrate 23 g • Fiber 5 g • Protein 5 g

Loong Poong Salad

MARINADE

1	cup sugar
1	cup vegetable oil
1/2	cup vinegar
2	tablespoons dry mustard
1	teaspoon salt
1 1/2	cups water

SALAD

1	(16-ounce) package frozen whole kernel corn, thawed
1	(16-ounce) package frozen green peas, thawed
2	(8-ounce) cans sliced water chestnuts, drained
8	ounces mushrooms, sliced
8	ounces bean sprouts
1	cup sliced celery
1	green bell pepper, julienned
1	(2-ounce) jar diced pimento, drained

For the marinade, combine the sugar, oil, vinegar, dry mustard, salt and water in a large bowl and stir until the sugar is dissolved.

For the salad, add the corn, peas, water chestnuts, mushrooms, bean sprouts, celery, bell pepper and pimento to the marinade and mix well. Marinate, covered, in the refrigerator for several hours or overnight. Drain in a colander before serving.

Makes 12 servings

One of the first gala celebrations was held on the day Mesa County was created in 1883. A parade and bonfire highlighted the event.

—Mesa County Colorado: A 100-Year History

Per serving

Calories 320 • Fat 20 g • Cholesterol 0 mg • Sodium 240 mg • Carbohydrate 35 g • Fiber 5 g • Protein 5 g

Red Potato Salad

3 pounds new red potatoes (or other potato variety of choice)

5 to 6 tablespoons sugar

12 hard-cooked eggs, sliced

1 medium onion, diced

3 cups mayonnaise-style salad dressing

2 tablespoons mustard

Cook the potatoes in water to cover in a large saucepan until tender. Drain the water and place the potatoes on a large baking sheet. Break the potatoes into large chunks and sprinkle with the sugar. Let stand for about 15 minutes. Combine the potatoes, hard-cooked eggs and onion in a large bowl. Stir together the salad dressing and mustard in a small bowl. Add the dressing to the potato mixture and mix well. Refrigerate, covered, for several hours or overnight. Note: This is a good base salad for your favorite ingredients.

Makes 24 (1/2-cup) servings

Sponsored By
Christi's Interiors

Per serving

Calories 240 • Fat 17 g • Cholesterol 115 mg • Sodium 240 mg • Carbohydrate 18 g • Fiber 1 g • Protein 5 g

Asparagus Bundles

16 asparagus spears
4   thin slices prosciutto
1/2 cup shredded fontina cheese
    Cumin seeds

Bring enough water to cover the asparagus spears to a boil in a large saucepan or skillet. Add the asparagus and cook until tender-crisp; drain. Arrange 4 asparagus spears together to make a bundle. Repeat to make 4 bundles. Wrap each bundle with a slice of prosciutto. Arrange the bundles on a broiler pan. Top each with the cheese and sprinkle with the cumin seeds. Broil until the cheese melts. Serve warm.

Makes 4 servings

Per serving
Calories 110 • Fat 7 g • Cholesterol 25 mg • Sodium 270 mg • Carbohydrate 3 g • Fiber 2 g • Protein 7 g

Apple Baked Beans

2   (31-ounce) cans baked beans
3/4 cup packed brown sugar
3/4 cup light molasses, or 1/2 cup
    dark molasses
5   slices bacon, chopped
1/2 cup ketchup
1   medium onion, chopped
1   tart apple (Granny Smith), diced

Combine the beans, brown sugar, molasses, bacon, ketchup, onion and unpeeled apple in a bowl and mix well. Spoon into a 2-quart baking dish. Bake, uncovered, at 325 degrees for 2 hours. Note: The beans may also be heated in a slow cooker on Low for 6 to 8 hours. Serve with grilled burgers, ribs, chicken or steak.

Makes 12 servings

Per serving
Calories 320 • Fat 4.5 g • Cholesterol 5 mg • Sodium 600 mg • Carbohydrate 61 g • Fiber 8 g • Protein 11 g

Fuzla Beans

In 1939 the four Prinster brothers expanded their "City Market" operation into the Western Slope's first "supermarket," now a part of a major chain.

—Mesa County Colorado: A 100-Year History

5	tablespoons (about) vegetable oil
3	onions, chopped
2	garlic cloves, chopped
1	green bell pepper, julienned
1	(15-ounce) can kidney beans
1	(15-ounce) can pinto beans
1	(15-ounce) can cannellini beans
1	(14-ounce) can diced tomatoes
1	bay leaf
1	tablespoon basil (fresh or dried)
1	tablespoon curry powder
1	tablespoon paprika
1	tablespoon oregano (optional)
	Chili powder to taste (optional)
	Salt to taste

Heat the oil in a large saucepan and add the onions. Cook until the onions are tender. Add the garlic and bell pepper and cook for 5 to 10 minutes, stirring occasionally. Add the beans, tomatoes, bay leaf, basil, curry powder, paprika, oregano, chili powder and salt. Bring to a boil; reduce the heat. Cover and simmer for 10 minutes. Remove the bay leaf. Serve with crusty bread or pita bread. Garnish with sour cream or plain yogurt and shredded cheese.

Makes 10 servings

Sponsored By

Lizzy's Logos Embroidery

Per serving

Calories 200 • Fat 7 g • Cholesterol 0 mg • Sodium 690 mg • Carbohydrate 28 g • Fiber 8 g • Protein 9 g

Citrus-Glazed Carrots

4 cups baby carrots

1 (14-ounce) jar preserved kumquats

2 tablespoons brown sugar

Grated zest of 1 orange

1 tablespoon orange juice

1 tablespoon honey

1 tablespoon butter, melted

1/2 teaspoon salt

Bring enough water to cover the carrots to a boil in a large saucepan or skillet. Add the carrots and cook until tender-crisp; drain. Drain the kumquats, reserving 1/3 cup of the liquid. Combine the reserved liquid and remaining ingredients in a bowl and mix well. Place the carrots and kumquats in a shallow 1 1/2-quart baking dish. Pour the honey mixture over the carrots. Bake at 350 degrees for 20 minutes or until heated through.

Makes 8 servings

Per serving

Calories 130 • Fat 2 g • Cholesterol 5 mg • Sodium 240 mg • Carbohydrate 29 g • Fiber 1 g • Protein 1 g

Chile Cheese Corn Casserole

2 eggs

2 (15-ounce) cans cream-style corn

3/4 cup yellow cornmeal

1/2 teaspoon baking powder

1/4 cup canola oil

2 (4-ounce) cans chopped green chiles

8 ounces sharp Cheddar cheese, shredded

Whisk the eggs in a medium bowl. Whisk in the corn, cornmeal, baking powder and canola oil until well blended. Stir together the chiles and cheese. Spread half the corn mixture in a 9x13-inch baking pan coated with nonstick cooking spray. Top with half the cheese mixture. Repeat the layers. Bake at 350 degrees for 45 minutes.

Makes 8 servings

Per serving

Calories 220 • Fat 12 g • Cholesterol 55 mg • Sodium 560 mg • Carbohydrate 21 g • Fiber 1 g • Protein 8 g

Mushroom Casserole

2 1/2 pounds mushrooms, sliced
1/2 cup butter (1 stick) or margarine
8 to 10 slices bread
6 tablespoons butter or margarine, softened
1 cup chopped celery
1 cup chopped onion
1 cup chopped green bell pepper
2 cups mayonnaise
4 eggs
2 cups 2% milk
2 (10-ounce) cans cream of mushroom soup
1 teaspoon salt
1/2 teaspoon pepper
1/2 cup bread crumbs or grated Parmesan cheese

Sauté the mushrooms in 1/2 cup butter in a large skillet over high heat until golden brown, stirring frequently. Spread 1 side of each bread slice with about 2 teaspoons butter. Cut the bread slices into 1-inch squares. Place half the bread in a 9×13-inch baking dish coated with nonstick cooking spray. Top with half the mushrooms. Combine the celery, onion, bell pepper and mayonnaise in a bowl and mix well. Spread half the mayonnaise mixture over the mushrooms. Repeat the layers. Whisk together the eggs, milk, soup, salt and pepper in a bowl until well blended. Pour over the layers. Refrigerate, covered, overnight. Sprinkle with the bread crumbs. Bake, covered, at 325 degrees for 50 minutes; uncover. Bake for 10 to 15 minutes longer or until browned. Note: This is an excellent accompaniment to roasted meats.

Makes 10 servings

Per serving
Calories 640 • Fat 56 g • Cholesterol 150 mg • Sodium 1170 mg • Carbohydrate 24 g • Fiber 2 g • Protein 8 g

Hash Brown Potato Casserole

1   (32-ounce) package frozen hash
    brown potatoes, thawed
1   (10-ounce) can cream of chicken soup
1   cup milk
1   cup sour cream
1/2 cup (1 stick) butter, melted
2   cups (8 ounces) shredded sharp
    Cheddar cheese
1/2 cup chopped onion
1   teaspoon salt
1/4 teaspoon pepper
2   cups cornflakes, crushed
1/4 cup (1/2 stick) butter, melted

Combine the potatoes, soup, milk, sour cream, 1/2 cup butter, cheese, onion, salt and pepper in a large bowl and mix well. Spoon into a 9×13-inch baking dish. Top with the cornflakes and drizzle with 1/4 cup butter. Bake at 350 degrees for 45 minutes.

Makes 8 servings

Sponsored By

Julie Butherus

Re/Max 4000, Inc.

Per serving

Calories 490 • Fat 33 g • Cholesterol 90 mg • Sodium 1010 mg • Carbohydrate 36 g • Fiber 2 g • Protein 13 g

Pacific Rim Mashed Potatoes

MASHED POTATOES

2	pounds potatoes, peeled and cubed
1 1/2	teaspoons salt
1	teaspoon unsalted butter
1/2	teaspoon minced garlic, or to taste
2	tablespoons unsalted butter
1	cup milk
	Thai Peanut Sauce (page 65)
	Salt and pepper to taste

Potatoes were planted early on the Western Slope. . . .Other potato growing regions included Fruita and Loma west of Grand Junction, known for early potatoes.

—A Land Alone: Colorado's Western Slope

For the mashed potatoes, combine the potatoes, 1 1/2 teaspoons salt and enough water to cover the potatoes in a saucepan and bring to a boil. Reduce the heat to medium and cook for about 15 minutes or until the potatoes are tender. Drain the potatoes and place in an ovenproof bowl. Whip with an electric mixer until smooth. Place the potatoes in a preheated 300-degree oven for 2 to 3 minutes to evaporate the excess moisture. Melt 1 teaspoon butter in a small skillet and add the garlic. Sauté the garlic over low heat for about 15 seconds. Stir the garlic into the potatoes. Combine 2 tablespoons butter, milk and 1/4 to 1/2 cup of the Thai Peanut Sauce in a large saucepan and bring to a boil. Add the potatoes and beat for about 2 minutes or until thoroughly combined. Season with salt and pepper.

Makes 8 servings

Per serving
Calories 140 • Fat 4 g • Cholesterol 10 mg • Sodium 460 mg • Carbohydrate 22 g • Fiber 1 g • Protein 4 g
Per serving Thai Peanut Sauce
Calories 360 • Fat 28 g • Cholesterol 0 mg • Sodium 1000 mg • Carbohydrate 23 g • Fiber 4 g • Protein 9 g

THAI PEANUT SAUCE

2	cups canned unsweetened coconut milk
1/2	cup creamy peanut butter
1/4	cup packed brown sugar
1/4	cup soy sauce
1	tablespoon unseasoned rice vinegar
1	cup julienned fresh Thai basil
1/4	cup red curry paste
1/2	onion, chopped
2	tablespoons minced garlic
1	tablespoon minced lemon grass
1 1/2	cups chopped fresh cilantro

For the peanut sauce, combine the coconut milk, peanut butter, brown sugar, soy sauce, vinegar, basil, curry paste, onion, garlic, lemon grass and cilantro in a saucepan and mix well. Cook over low heat, until the sauce begins to thicken and the oils from the curry come to the surface, stirring constantly (do not boil). Taste and adjust seasonings with additional brown sugar, soy sauce or vinegar. Let cool.

Makes 8 servings

Campfire Potatoes

8	cups sliced potatoes (about 3 1/2 pounds)
1	cup chopped green bell pepper
2	medium onions, sliced and separated into rings
3	cups (12 ounces) shredded Cheddar cheese
4	slices bacon, crisp-cooked and crumbled Pepper

Fold each of two 36-inch pieces of heavy-duty foil in half to make a double thickness; spray with nonstick cooking spray. Layer 1/4 of the potatoes, 1/2 of the bell pepper, 1/2 onions, 1/4 of the cheese, the remaining potatoes and 1/4 of the cheese on each foil piece. Top with the bacon. Sprinkle with pepper. Form packets by bringing up opposite sides of the foil; seal with a double fold and vent. Cook the packets over medium indirect heat in a covered grill for 30 to 35 minutes or until the potatoes are tender.

Makes 8 servings   Per serving

Calories 290 • Fat 19 g • Cholesterol 50 mg • Sodium 360 mg • Carbohydrate 15 g • Fiber 2 g • Protein 14 g

Roasted Potatoes with Garlic, Lemon and Oregano

3   pounds baking potatoes, peeled and cut into 1 1/2-inch cubes
1/2   cup olive oil
4   garlic cloves, minced
1 1/2   teaspoons dried oregano, crushed
1   teaspoon salt
    Freshly ground pepper to taste
1/2   cup beef stock or chicken stock
1/3   cup fresh lemon juice
2   to 3 tablespoons chopped fresh oregano

Place the potatoes in a single layer in a 9×13-inch baking dish. Pour the olive oil over the potatoes. Add the garlic, dried oregano, salt and pepper and toss to coat. Bake the potatoes at 400 degrees for 15 minutes. Add the stock and mix well. Bake for 10 minutes longer. Stir in the lemon juice. Bake for 10 to 15 minutes longer or until the potatoes are tender. To brown the potatoes, broil for 2 to 3 minutes. Sprinkle with the fresh oregano and serve immediately.

Makes 6 servings

Per serving
Calories 360 • Fat 19 g • Cholesterol 0 mg • Sodium 390 mg • Carbohydrate 44 g • Fiber 3 g • Protein 6 g

Rosemary Reds

2   to 4 tablespoons olive oil
12   medium red potatoes, quartered (about 3 pounds)
6   garlic cloves
3   tablespoons (or more) fresh rosemary leaves, finely chopped
    Kosher salt to taste
    Coarsely ground pepper to taste

Pour the olive oil into a 10×15-inch baking pan with sides. Add the remaining ingredients and toss to coat. Separate the potatoes into a single layer. Bake the potatoes at 400 degrees for 45 minutes or until brown and tender, stirring frequently. Spoon into a serving bowl and serve immediately.

Makes 6 to 8 servings

Per serving
Calories 130 • Fat 4 g • Cholesterol 0 mg • Sodium 160 mg • Carbohydrate 22 g • Fiber 2 g • Protein 3 g

Twice-Baked Potatoes

3   baking potatoes
    Vegetable oil
1/2 cup (1 stick) butter, melted
1/2 cup cream
1/2 cup sour cream
1/2 cup sliced green onions
1   cup (4 ounces) shredded
    Cheddar cheese
    Salt and pepper to taste

Rub the potatoes with oil. Bake at 400 degrees for 1 hour to 1 hour and 20 minutes. Cut each potato in half lengthwise. Scoop the potato pulp from each half, leaving about 1/8 inch of potato next to the skin. Place the potato pulp in a bowl, reserving the potato skins. Add the remaining ingredients to the potato pulp and mix well. Spoon 1/6 of the mixture into each potato skin and place on a baking sheet. Bake at 350 degrees for 20 to 30 minutes.

Makes 6 servings

Per serving
Calories 360 • Fat 28 g • Cholesterol 80 mg • Sodium 630 mg • Carbohydrate 17 g • Fiber 1 g • Protein 8 g

Golden Squash Soufflé

3   pounds yellow squash, cooked and
    mashed
2   eggs, beaten
1/2 cup chopped onion
1   tablespoon sugar
1   teaspoon salt
1/2 teaspoon pepper
1/2 cup (1 stick) margarine, melted
1/2 cup cracker meal

Whisk together the squash, eggs, onion, sugar, salt and pepper in a bowl until well blended. Pour into a greased 1 1/2-quart baking dish. Drizzle with the margarine. Sprinkle the cracker meal over the top. Bake at 375 degrees for 1 hour or until the top is browned.

Makes 10 servings

Per serving
Calories 90 • Fat 5 g • Cholesterol 20 mg • Sodium 190 mg • Carbohydrate 9 g • Fiber 2 g • Protein 2 g

Ranch Mac 'n' Cheese

The National Municipal League and Look Magazine named Grand Junction an All-American City in 1963 for the most beautiful development of a downtown.

—Mesa County Colorado: A 100-Year History

1	cup milk
1/4	cup (1/2 stick) butter or margarine
2	envelopes ranch salad dressing mix
1	teaspoon garlic powder
1	teaspoon garlic salt
1	teaspoon lemon pepper
4	ounces Colby cheese, cubed
4	ounces Monterey Jack cheese, cubed
8	ounces sour cream
1/2	cup crushed saltines
16	ounces elbow macaroni, cooked and drained
2	tablespoons grated Parmesan cheese

Combine the milk, butter, ranch dressing mix, garlic powder, garlic salt, lemon pepper, Colby cheese and Monterey Jack cheese in a Dutch oven or large heavy saucepan. Cook over medium heat until the cheeses are melted and the mixture begins to thicken, stirring constantly. Fold in the sour cream. Add the saltines and the macaroni and mix well. Cook until heated through, stirring frequently. Pour into a serving dish. Sprinkle with the Parmesan cheese.

Makes 8 servings

Sponsored By

Nannette and Bill Lintott

Per serving

Calories 420 • Fat 30 g • Cholesterol 75 mg • Sodium 890 mg • Carbohydrate 24 g • Fiber 1 g • Protein 12 g

Rice Casserole Supreme

3   cups rice

1   cup chopped parsley

1/2   cup (2 ounces) shredded
      Cheddar cheese

1/3   cup chopped green bell pepper

1/4   cup chopped onion

2   garlic cloves, minced

2   eggs

1   (12-ounce) can evaporated milk

1/2   cup vegetable oil
      Grated zest and juice of 1 lemon

1/2   teaspoon salt

1/2   teaspoon seasoned salt

1/2   teaspoon pepper
      Paprika

Cook the rice according to the package directions. Combine the cooked rice, parsley, cheese, bell pepper, onion and garlic in a large bowl and mix well. Whisk the eggs in a medium bowl. Whisk in the evaporated milk, oil, lemon zest and juice, salt, seasoned salt and pepper until blended. Stir into the rice mixture and mix well. Spoon into a greased 2-quart casserole. Sprinkle with paprika. Bake at 350 degrees for 45 minutes or until a knife inserted near the center comes out clean.

Makes 10 servings

Per serving

Calories 250 • Fat 17 g • Cholesterol 60 mg • Sodium 280 mg • Carbohydrate 19 g • Fiber 1 g • Protein 7 g

Colorful Fried Rice

1	tablespoon peanut oil
1	large garlic clove, minced
1	cup sliced Napa cabbage
6	ounces snow peas (pea pods), julienned
1	red bell pepper, julienned
2	carrots, julienned
2	green onions, diagonally sliced
1/2	small onion, sliced
1	tablespoon peanut oil
1	egg, beaten
2	cups cooked rice, chilled
3	tablespoons soy sauce

Heat 1 tablespoon peanut oil in a wok or large nonstick skillet and add the garlic. Stir in the cabbage, snow peas, bell pepper, carrots, green onions and onion. Stir-fry for 2 minutes or until the vegetables are tender-crisp. Remove the vegetables from the pan. Pour about 1/2 tablespoon peanut oil into the wok and heat. Pour the egg into the pan, quickly tilting the pan to spread the egg and form a thin omelet (do not stir). Cut the omelet into strips and remove from the pan. Pour the remaining 1/2 tablespoon peanut oil into the wok and add the rice. Cook and stir until heated through. Return the stir-fried vegetables and omelet strips to the pan and heat through. Stir in the soy sauce and mix well.

Makes 4 servings

Per serving

Calories 260 • Fat 11 g • Cholesterol 55 mg • Sodium 810 mg • Carbohydrate 35 g • Fiber 3 g • Protein 7 g

Cold Cucumber Soup

3   cucumbers

2   tablespoons butter

1   leek (white part only), sliced

1   bay leaf

1   tablespoon all-purpose flour

3   cups chicken stock

1   teaspoon salt

1   cup heavy cream

     Juice from 1/2 lemon

     Sour cream

1   teaspoon chopped fresh dill weed or mint leaves

Peel, seed and slice 2 of the cucumbers. Set aside the remaining cucumber. Sauté the sliced cucumbers in the butter with the leek and bay leaf in a large skillet over medium heat for about 20 minutes or until tender. Stir in the flour until blended. Add the stock and salt and mix well. Simmer for 30 minutes. Remove the bay leaf. Ladle the mixture, in batches, into a blender or food processor and purée. Strain and chill. About 1 hour before serving, peel, seed and shred the reserved cucumber. Add the shredded cucumber, cream and lemon juice to the cucumber purée; chill. To serve, ladle into individual cups and top with dollops of sour cream. Sprinkle with the dill.

Makes 5 servings

Tourism, which one can trace all the way back to the 1860s, spread like wildfire in the 1950s and 1960s and became one of the top three industries of the region.

—A Land Alone: Colorado's Western Slope

Sponsored By

The Walck Family

Per serving

Calories 300 • Fat 24 g • Cholesterol 80 mg • Sodium 1560 mg • Carbohydrate 16 g • Fiber 2 g • Protein 7 g

Cream of Zucchini Soup

1 medium onion, chopped
1/2 cup (1 stick) butter
3 or 4 medium zucchini, chopped
(about 1 pound)
1/2 cup all-purpose flour
1 teaspoon salt
1/4 teaspoon white pepper
2 (14-ounce) cans chicken broth
2 cups half-and-half
Dash of cayenne pepper, or to taste

Sauté the onion in the butter in a large saucepan until the onion is translucent. Add the zucchini and cook until tender. Stir in the flour, salt and white pepper until blended. Stir in the broth gradually and mix well. Cook until thickened, stirring constantly. Reduce the heat to low; simmer, covered, for 5 to 10 minutes. Stir in the half-and-half. Ladle the mixture, in batches, into a blender and purée. (Remove the center part of the blender lid and cover with a towel. Blend at low speed until mixed. Then blend at high speed until smooth.) Pour the puréed mixture into a large bowl. Return the mixture to the saucepan and heat through. Season with the cayenne pepper. Stir before serving.

Makes 8 servings

Sponsored By
Quick Temps

Per serving
Calories 240 • Fat 19 g • Cholesterol 50 mg • Sodium 650 mg • Carbohydrate 13 g • Fiber 1 g • Protein 5 g

Simple and Savory Vegetable Soup

1   medium onion, chopped
2   tablespoons butter
2   or 3 carrots, chopped
1   (14-ounce) can chicken broth
1   cup chopped zucchini
    Kernels of 1 ear of corn
1   medium tomato, chopped
    Pinch of thyme, or to taste
    Chopped parsley
    Salt and pepper to taste

Sauté the onion in the butter in a saucepan until tender. Add the carrots and broth and bring to a boil. Reduce the heat; simmer for about 8 minutes. Add the zucchini, corn kernels, tomato, thyme, parsley, salt and pepper. Simmer for 5 to 8 minutes longer or until the vegetables are tender-crisp.

Makes 2 servings

The choicest of all the farming and ranching locations on the Western Slope lay at the junction of the Colorado and Gunnison rivers. . . .The first ranch appeared on September 10 [1882] and the town of Grand Junction, initially named Ute, was located on September 26.

—A Land Alone: Colorado's Western Slope

Per serving
Calories 270 • Fat 13 g • Cholesterol 30 mg • Sodium 1290 mg • Carbohydrate 35 g • Fiber 6 g • Protein 8 g

Avgolemono (Chicken and Rice Soup)

1 (3-pound) stewing chicken, cut into quarters
1 onion, sliced
1 carrot, sliced
1 rib celery, sliced
1 bay leaf
  Salt and pepper to taste
3 egg whites
3 egg yolks
  Juice of 1 lemon, strained
1 teaspoon dill weed
1 cup rice, cooked

Place the chicken in a stockpot and add enough water to cover. Bring to a boil and simmer for 15 minutes, skimming off the foam. Add the onion, carrot, celery and bay leaf; simmer for about 1 1/2 hours or until the chicken falls away from the bones. Remove the chicken and cool. Discard the bones. Shred the chicken breasts and set aside. Cover and refrigerate the remaining chicken for another use. Strain the stock through a sieve lined with cheesecloth. Return the stock to the stockpot and season with salt and pepper. (There should be 6 to 8 cups stock.) Whisk or beat the egg whites in a large bowl until stiff. Whisk in the egg yolks 1 at a time. Stir in the lemon juice slowly and mix well. Gradually stir about 2 cups of the stock into the egg mixture, beating constantly. Stir the egg mixture back into the stock. Add the shredded chicken, dill and rice. Simmer for 3 to 4 minutes or until thickened and heated through (do not boil).

Makes 6 to 8 servings

Per serving
Calories 110 • Fat 3 g • Cholesterol 120 mg • Sodium 60 mg • Carbohydrate 12 g • Fiber 1 g • Protein 9 g

Santa Fe Chicken Soup

6 cups water

6 boneless skinless chicken thighs

1 cup tomato juice

1 teaspoon cumin

1 teaspoon Mexican oregano

1/2 onion, chopped

1 teaspoon chopped fresh garlic

2 tomatoes, chopped

2 tablespoons chopped jalapeño chiles

2 tablespoons chopped fresh cilantro

1/4 cup chopped green chiles

1/4 teaspoon red pepper flakes

2 cups heavy cream

1/2 cup chicken base paste

Bring the water to a boil in a large saucepan. Add the chicken. Simmer until the chicken is cooked through. Remove the chicken, reserving the cooking liquid. Cut the chicken into bite-size pieces and return to the cooking liquid. Add the tomato juice, cumin, oregano, onion, garlic, tomatoes, jalapeño chiles, cilantro, green chiles and red pepper flakes. Bring to a boil and boil for 10 minutes. Add the cream. Bring to a boil and immediately whisk in the chicken base paste. Adjust the seasonings to taste.

Makes 6 to 8 servings

From

Main Street Café

Per serving

Calories 470 • Fat 39 g • Cholesterol 165 mg • Sodium 3470 mg • Carbohydrate 14 g • Fiber 2 g • Protein 17 g

Fall

Entrées

Fall Menu

Onion Soufflé
page 38

Perked Cider
page 150

Mixed Greens with Spiced Pears and Almonds
page 49

Macadamia Nut-Encrusted Halibut with Sun-Dried Tomato Cream Sauce
page 101

Pumpkin Pie
page 133

Beef Bourguignon Fillet

1 (3-pound) beef tenderloin,
   well trimmed, cut crosswise into
   1-inch-thick slices
   Kosher salt to taste
   Freshly ground pepper to taste
3 tablespoons olive oil
2 to 4 slices bacon, diced
3 garlic cloves, minced
1¼ cups Burgundy
2¼ cups beef stock
2 sprigs of fresh thyme
1 teaspoon salt
½ teaspoon freshly ground pepper
1 tablespoon tomato paste
1½ cups pearl onions
10 carrots, cut diagonally into
   1-inch pieces
¼ cup (½ stick) butter, softened
2 tablespoons all-purpose flour
8 ounces mushrooms, sliced
1 tablespoon butter
1 tablespoon olive oil

Season the beef slices on both sides with salt and pepper. Sear in 3 tablespoons olive oil in a large heavy skillet over medium-high heat for 2 to 3 minutes per side. Remove the beef to a platter. Sauté the bacon in the same skillet over medium-low heat for about 5 minutes or until browned and crisp. Drain the bacon on a paper towel. Discard all but 2 tablespoons of the drippings. Add the garlic to the reserved drippings and cook for 30 seconds. Add the wine and cook over high heat for 1 minute, scraping the bottom and side of the skillet. Add the next 5 ingredients. Bring to a boil; cook over medium-high heat for 10 minutes. Strain the sauce and return to the skillet. Add the onions and carrots; simmer for 20 to 30 minutes or until the sauce is reduced and the vegetables are tender. Make a paste of ¼ cup butter and the flour; blend into the sauce. Simmer for 2 minutes or until thickened. Sauté the mushrooms in 1 tablespoon butter and 1 tablespoon olive oil in a skillet over high heat until browned and tender. Add the beef slices, bacon and mushrooms to the sauce. Cook, covered, over low heat for 7 to 10 minutes or until heated through.

Makes 8 servings

Per serving

Calories 420 • Fat 16 g • Cholesterol 95 mg • Sodium 510 mg • Carbohydrate 21 g • Fiber 3 g • Protein 38 g

Filet Mignon with Shiitake Mushroom Sauce

1 1/2 tablespoons margarine or butter

1 cup finely chopped shallots

1 1/2 pounds shiitake mushrooms, stems removed

3 cups dry red wine

3 (10-ounce) cans beef consommé (3 3/4 cups)

12 (4-ounce) beef tenderloin steaks (about 1 inch thick)
  Cracked pepper to taste

1 1/2 tablespoons margarine or butter

1 1/2 cups dry red wine

3 tablespoons low-sodium soy sauce

2 tablespoons cornstarch

3 tablespoons chopped fresh thyme, or 1 tablespoon dried thyme

Melt 1 1/2 tablespoons margarine in a large nonstick skillet coated with nonstick cooking spray over medium heat. Add the shallots and mushrooms and sauté for 4 minutes. Add 3 cups wine and 2 1/4 cups of the consommé; simmer for 5 minutes, stirring frequently. Remove the mushrooms with a slotted spoon to a large bowl. Increase the heat to high and cook the wine mixture for 5 minutes or until reduced to 1 1/2 cups. Add the wine mixture to the mushrooms. Wipe the skillet with a paper towel. Season the steaks with the pepper. Melt 1 1/2 tablespoons margarine in the skillet over medium heat. Add the steaks and cook for 3 minutes per side. Reduce the heat to medium-low and cook for 1 1/2 minutes per side or to desired degree of doneness. Remove the steaks to a platter and keep warm. Pour 1 1/2 cups wine and the remaining consommé into the skillet. Bring to a boil; cook for 1 minute, scraping the bottom and side of skillet. Blend the soy sauce and cornstarch in a small bowl. Add the mushroom mixture, cornstarch mixture and the thyme to the skillet. Bring to a boil; cook for 1 minute, stirring constantly. Serve the mushroom sauce with the steaks.

Makes 12 servings

Per serving

Calories 250 • Fat 7 g • Cholesterol 60 mg • Sodium 1250 mg • Carbohydrate 17 g • Fiber 1 g • Protein 27 g

Oven-Barbecued Brisket

1 (4- to 5-pound) beef brisket, trimmed
1 teaspoon celery salt
1 teaspoon garlic salt
1 teaspoon onion salt
2 teaspoons liquid smoke
  Salt and pepper to taste
3 tablespoons Worcestershire sauce
1/2 cup ketchup
1/4 cup water
1/4 cup packed brown sugar
1 small onion, chopped
1 tablespoon chili powder
1 tablespoon vinegar
1 tablespoon Worcestershire sauce
1/2 teaspoon pepper
1/2 teaspoon Tabasco sauce

Place the brisket in a large sealable plastic bag or large bowl. Combine the celery salt, garlic salt and onion salt and sprinkle over the brisket. Sprinkle the liquid smoke over the brisket. Marinate, covered, in the refrigerator overnight. Place the brisket in a large roasting pan. Season with salt and pepper and 3 tablespoons Worcestershire sauce. Cover tightly with foil. Bake at 250 degrees for 8 hours. Remove the brisket from the pan and discard the drippings. Cool the brisket and slice. Meanwhile, combine the ketchup, water, brown sugar, onion, chili powder, vinegar, 1 tablespoon Worcestershire sauce, 1/2 teaspoon pepper and Tabasco sauce in a saucepan and simmer for 10 minutes. Return the sliced brisket to the roasting pan and pour the barbecue sauce over the meat. Bake, uncovered, at 250 degrees for 30 minutes. Note: This dish freezes well.

Makes 12 servings

Throughout much of the Western Slope, good ranch land was transformed into subdivisions in the 1960s and 1970s. One could hardly blame the ranchers. After surviving the Depression and experiencing low cattle prices more often than not, they were offered insane, unbelievable prices for their land. . . . If real estate developers were not pressuring ranchers and other owners to sell with the lure of instant gold, coal companies, chain-stores, and recreation industries were.

—A Land Alone: Colorado's Western Slope

Per serving
Calories 330• Fat 13 g • Cholesterol 130 mg • Sodium 450 mg • Carbohydrate 9 g • Fiber 0 g • Protein 43 g

Steaks with Garlic-Wasabi Sauce

STEAKS

1/2	cup fresh bread crumbs
2	tablespoons chopped parsley
2	garlic cloves, minced
2	tablespoons butter
2	onions, thinly sliced
4	(8-ounce) beef tenderloin steaks (about 1 1/2 inches thick)
	Salt and pepper to taste
	Garlic-Wasabi Sauce (page 83)
5	tablespoons cold butter

The Stockman's Ball and Banquet is an annual event sponsored by the Plateau Valley Stockgrowers Association, founded in 1902.

—Mesa County Colorado: A 100-Year History

For the steaks, combine the bread crumbs, parsley and garlic in a small bowl and set aside. Melt 2 tablespoons butter in a large heavy skillet over medium-low heat. Add the onions and sauté for about 15 minutes or until tender and golden brown. Meanwhile, season the steaks with salt and pepper and arrange on a broiler pan. Broil to desired doneness (about 4 minutes per side for medium-rare). Sprinkle the crumb mixture over the steaks. Broil for about 2 minutes longer or until the crumbs are golden brown. Pour the Garlic-Wasabi Sauce into a medium saucepan and bring to a simmer. Remove from the heat. Whisk 5 tablespoons butter gradually into the sauce until melted. Arrange 1/4 of the onions in the center of each of 4 individual serving plates. Top each with a steak. Spoon the sauce around the steaks and serve.

GARLIC-WASABI SAUCE

2	cups canned low-salt chicken broth
1	cup canned beef broth
1/2	cup chopped onion
1/4	cup chopped peeled apple
1/4	cup chopped carrots
1/4	cup chopped celery
1/4	cup chopped seeded tomato
1	tablespoon soy sauce
3	garlic cloves, chopped
1	teaspoon tomato paste
5	teaspoons wasabi powder (dried Japanese horseradish)
5	teaspoons water
	Salt and pepper to taste

For the sauce, combine the chicken broth, beef broth, onion, apple, carrots, celery, tomato, soy sauce, garlic and tomato paste in a large saucepan and bring to a boil; reduce the heat. Simmer, covered, for 1 hour. Strain the liquid into a medium saucepan. Bring to a boil; cook for about 15 minutes or until reduced to 1/2 cup. Stir the wasabi powder into the water until dissolved and let stand for 5 minutes. Stir the wasabi mixture into the sauce until blended. Season with salt and pepper. Note: The sauce can be made 1 day ahead. Store, covered, in the refrigerator.

Makes 4 servings

From

Blue Moon

Per serving

Calories 580 • Fat 30 g • Cholesterol 175 mg • Sodium 1080 mg • Carbohydrate 26 g • Fiber 4 g • Protein 52 g

Taco-Filled Peppers

1   pound ground beef

1   envelope taco seasoning mix

1   (8-ounce) can kidney beans, drained and rinsed

1   cup salsa

4   green bell peppers

1   tomato, chopped

1/2   cup (2 ounces) shredded Cheddar cheese

1/2   cup sour cream

Brown the ground beef in a large skillet, stirring until crumbly; pour off the drippings. Add the taco seasoning mix, beans and salsa and mix well. Bring to a boil; reduce the heat and simmer for 5 minutes. Cut the bell peppers in half lengthwise and discard the stems and seeds. Blanch the peppers in boiling water in a large saucepan for 3 minutes. Drain on paper towels. Spoon about 1/2 cup of the ground beef mixture into each pepper half. Place the peppers in an ungreased 9×13-inch baking dish. Bake, covered, at 350 degrees for 15 to 20 minutes or until the peppers are tender-crisp and the filling is heated through. Top each pepper with tomato, cheese and sour cream before serving.

Makes 4 servings

Sponsored By

Kim Jones

Per serving

Calories 530 • Fat 33 g • Cholesterol 115 mg • Sodium 960 mg • Carbohydrate 25 g • Fiber 4 g • Protein 28 g

Veal Forestière

6   veal cutlets
1/2   cup (1 stick) butter or margarine
16   ounces mushrooms, finely chopped
1   tablespoon finely chopped shallots
1   tablespoon dry vermouth
1/2   teaspoon cornstarch
1   cup sour cream

Sauté the veal in the butter in a large skillet until browned and cooked through. Remove the veal to a shallow baking dish. Sauté the mushrooms and shallots in the same skillet over medium-high heat until the liquid has evaporated, stirring frequently. Add the vermouth and cook for 1 minute, scraping the bottom and side of the skillet to loosen any browned bits. Stir the cornstarch into the sour cream until blended. Add the sour cream to the skillet and bring to a boil, stirring constantly. Pour the sauce over the veal. Bake at 350 degrees for 15 minutes or until heated through. Serve with pasta or rice.

Makes 6 servings

Sponsored By

Anne Nichols

Per serving

Calories 370 • Fat 26 g • Cholesterol 115 mg • Sodium 300 mg • Carbohydrate 5 g • Fiber 1 g • Protein 27 g

Roast Leg of Lamb

1 (5- to 6-pound) bone-in leg of lamb
6 garlic cloves, sliced
1 tablespoon dried oregano
1 tablespoon dried thyme
1 1/2 teaspoons dried savory or rosemary
  Salt and freshly ground pepper to taste
2 tablespoons olive oil
2 tablespoons butter, softened
1 cup (or more) chicken stock
  Juice of 2 lemons

The first deer hunting license was issued in 1903. Elk, deer, bobcat, and bear were plentiful, particularly in the DeBeque area.

—Mesa County Colorado: A 100-Year History

Make small cuts in the lamb with a sharp knife and insert the garlic slices. Combine the oregano, thyme, savory, salt and pepper with the olive oil and butter in a small bowl, stirring until blended. Rub the herb butter all over the lamb. Place the lamb in a large roasting pan. Roast at 325 degrees for about 3 hours (1/2 hour per pound) or until a meat thermometer inserted into the thickest part of the lamb registers 135 degrees. Combine the stock and lemon juice and use to baste the lamb during roasting. Remove the roast to a cutting board or platter; cover and let stand for 15 minutes. Slice and serve.

Makes 6 servings

Per serving
Calories 710 • Fat 32 g • Cholesterol 300 mg • Sodium 450 mg • Carbohydrate 5 g • Fiber 1 g • Protein 94 g

Pork Rib Roast with Milk Sauce

1/2 cup (1 stick) unsalted butter

2 carrots, chopped

2 ribs celery, chopped

1 medium onion, chopped

6 to 8 bay leaves

10 to 12 peppercorns

1 (6-pound) bone-in pork loin rib roast, trimmed

8 cups milk

Salt to taste

Melt the butter in a large heavy roasting pan and add the carrots, celery, onion, bay leaves and peppercorns. Cook for 5 to 10 minutes or until the onions are translucent. Add the roast and brown on all sides. Meanwhile, scald the milk in a saucepan. Add the milk to the roasting pan and season with salt. Roast, covered, at 400 degrees for 2 to 3 hours (20 minutes per pound) or until a meat thermometer registers 155 to 160 degrees. Remove the roast to a cutting board; cover and let stand for 15 minutes. Remove the bay leaves from the cooking liquid. Ladle the cooking liquid and vegetables, in batches, into a blender and purée. Taste the sauce and adjust the seasoning if needed. Slice the roast and serve with the sauce.

Makes 10 to 11 servings

From

il Bistro Italiano

Per serving

Calories 670 • Fat 35 g • Cholesterol 190 mg • Sodium 610 mg • Carbohydrate 12 g • Fiber 1 g • Protein 72 g

Marinated Pork Tenderloin

The hordes of tourists continued to cross the mountains in the 1970s. They never even broke stride. Some are hunters anxiously awaiting the deer and elk season in the fall.

—A Land Alone: Colorado's Western Slope

1/2 cup lemon juice

1/2 cup olive oil

1/2 cup wine vinegar

1/2 cup Worcestershire sauce

1/4 cup soy sauce

2 tablespoons dry mustard

1 tablespoon coarsely ground pepper

2 garlic cloves, crushed

1 1/2 teaspoons parsley flakes

3/4 teaspoon kosher salt

2 (3/4- to 1-pound) boneless pork tenderloins

Combine the lemon juice, olive oil, vinegar, Worcestershire sauce, soy sauce, dry mustard, pepper, garlic, parsley and salt in a large sealable plastic bag. Add the pork. Marinate in the refrigerator for several hours or overnight, turning the bag occasionally. Remove the pork from the marinade; discard the marinade. Grill the pork over hot coals for 8 to 10 minutes or until a meat thermometer registers 155 to 160 degrees, turning so all sides are evenly browned. Remove to a cutting board; cover and let stand for 10 minutes. Slice and serve.

Makes 6 servings

Sponsored By

Tom and Joan Graham

Per serving

Calories 400 • Fat 25 g • Cholesterol 100 mg • Sodium 1280 mg • Carbohydrate 9 g • Fiber 1 g • Protein 34 g

Pomegranate Pork Loin

PORK LOIN

1/4 cup extra-virgin olive oil

1/4 cup maple syrup

1/4 cup pomegranate juice

2 shallots, minced

Salt and pepper to taste

1 (3- to 4-pound) boneless pork loin roast

Pomegranate Sauce (below)

For the pork loin, combine the olive oil, maple syrup, pomegranate juice, shallots, salt and pepper in a large sealable plastic bag. Add the pork. Marinate in the refrigerator for 12 hours or overnight, turning the bag occasionally. Remove the pork from the marinade; discard the marinade. Place the pork in a roasting pan. Roast, covered, at 325 degrees for 1 hour. Uncover; roast for 1 hour longer or until a meat thermometer registers 155 to 160 degrees. Remove the pork to a cutting board; cover and let stand for 15 minutes. Slice the pork and serve with the Pomegranate Sauce. Garnish with pomegranate seeds.

POMEGRANATE SAUCE

1/4 cup packed brown sugar

1/4 cup pomegranate juice

3/4 cup water

1 tablespoon cornstarch

2 tablespoons Grand Marnier or other orange-flavored liqueur

For the sauce, combine the brown sugar, pomegranate juice and water in a small saucepan. Stir the cornstarch into the liqueur in a small bowl until blended; stir into the juice mixture. Bring to a boil; cook for 1 minute or until the mixture thickens, stirring constantly.

Makes 4 to 6 servings

Per serving

Calories 760 • Fat 26 g • Cholesterol 220 mg • Sodium 760 mg • Carbohydrate 57 g • Fiber 0 g • Protein 72 g

Honey Pecan Pork Cutlets

*On March 13, 1883,
Company F, Grand Valley
Guards, was mustered
into state service. It was
the first National Guard
Unit in Mesa County.*

—Mesa County Colorado:
A 100-Year History

4	boneless pork cutlets (1 pound)
1/2	cup (about) all-purpose flour
3	tablespoons butter
1/2	cup honey
1/4	cup chopped pecans, toasted

Coat the cutlets with the flour, shaking off any excess. Melt 1 tablespoon butter in a large heavy skillet over medium heat. Add the cutlets and brown on both sides. Stir the remaining 2 tablespoons butter, honey and pecans into the skillet. Simmer, covered, for 7 to 8 minutes or until the cutlets are done. Remove the cutlets to a serving platter. Stir the sauce and pour over the cutlets.

Makes 4 servings

Per serving

Calories 580 • Fat 30 g • Cholesterol 125 mg • Sodium 135 mg • Carbohydrate 47 g • Fiber 1 g • Protein 33 g

Spicy Green Chile Pork

1 1/4	pounds boneless pork loin
1	tablespoon olive oil
1	(29-ounce) can green chile strips, diced
1	(8-ounce) can diced tomatoes
1	(4-ounce) can diced jalapeño chiles
6	carrots, sliced (about 3 cups)
1/4	teaspoon white pepper
1/8	teaspoon each cumin, chicken bouillon granules, minced garlic and oregano Water
1/4	teaspoon salt, or to taste

Cut the pork into 1/2-inch pieces. Sauté the pork in the olive oil in a large skillet until browned on all sides. Spoon the pork into a very large saucepan or stockpot. Add the green chiles, tomatoes, jalapeños, carrots, pepper, cumin, bouillon granules, garlic and oregano and mix well. Add water to desired consistency. Season with salt. Simmer for at least 30 minutes, stirring occasionally.

Makes 8 servings

Per serving

Calories 150 • Fat 8 g • Cholesterol 45 mg • Sodium 560 mg • Carbohydrate 5 g • Fiber 1 g • Protein 14 g

Country-Style Oven Ribs

RIBS

1/2	teaspoon salt
1 1/2	teaspoons ground cumin
1	teaspoon paprika
1/2	teaspoon ground cinnamon
1/2	teaspoon pepper
1/4	teaspoon ground cloves
3 1/2	pounds country-style pork ribs
	Root Beer Basting Sauce (below)

ROOT BEER BASTING SAUCE

4	cups root beer (not low calorie)
1/3	cup barbecue sauce
2	tablespoons tomato sauce
1	tablespoon vinegar
2	teaspoons Dijon mustard
1	teaspoon Worcestershire sauce

For the ribs, combine the salt, cumin, paprika, cinnamon, pepper and cloves in a small bowl and rub over the ribs, coating completely. Place the ribs, bone side up, in a large shallow baking pan. Bake, covered, for 1 1/4 hours. Pour off any drippings. Turn the ribs meat side up. Spoon about half the basting sauce over the ribs. Bake, uncovered, for 45 minutes longer, basting once or twice with the basting sauce. Serve the ribs with the remaining sauce.

For the basting sauce, pour the root beer into a large saucepan and bring to a boil; reduce the heat. Simmer, uncovered, for 20 to 25 minutes or until reduced to 1 1/4 cups. Remove from the heat. Stir in the barbecue sauce, tomato sauce, vinegar, Dijon mustard and Worcestershire sauce. Bring to a boil; cook for 1 minute. Remove from the heat and set aside.

Makes 4 servings

[In the twenties,] Sentimentality, not cynicism, molded their lives. A family Christmas, a heaping table on Thanksgiving, a patriotic Fourth—all were hallowed traditions. . . .A tribute to mothers was published in Breckenridge's Summit County Journal: "But the greatest job in the world is the poorest paid in the matter of dollars and cents. The job of motherhood, the hardest work, the keenest mental anguish, the greatest physical pain, brings the smallest reward in wages."

—A Land Alone: Colorado's Western Slope

Per serving
Calories 1500 • Fat 118 g • Cholesterol 470 mg • Sodium 730 mg • Carbohydrate 5 g • Fiber 1 g • Protein 97 g

Double-Sauced Baby Back Ribs

3   racks baby back pork ribs
(about 4 pounds)

2   teaspoons (or more) seasoned salt

2   teaspoons (or more) garlic powder

2   teaspoons (or more) onion powder

2   teaspoons (or more) pepper

6   to 8 (or more) garlic cloves, chopped

2   (32-ounce) bottles barbecue sauce
(preferably KC Masterpiece Original)

1   (12-ounce) can (or more) beer

Cut the ribs into 2- to 3-rib portions. Combine the seasoned salt, garlic powder, onion powder and pepper and rub over the ribs, coating completely. Place in a covered container and marinate in the refrigerator for at least 1 hour. Combine the garlic, barbecue sauce and beer in a large stockpot or roasting pan and add the ribs. (A turkey cooker works well.) Cook over low heat for at least 1 hour. Remove the ribs and place directly over medium-hot coals with hickory chips. Grill for 5 minutes per side. Dunk the ribs back into the sauce; return to the grill and cook for 5 minutes per side. Repeat the dunking at least twice; grill until the ribs are tender and glazed.

Makes 6 servings

Sponsored By

Janet Hollingsworth

Per serving

Calories 1070 • Fat 70 g • Cholesterol 245 mg • Sodium 2590 mg • Carbohydrate 48 g • Fiber 0 g • Protein 51 g

Tagliatelle with Leek Sauce

2   sweet Italian sausages, casings removed
2   tablespoons olive oil
2   large leeks (white parts only), cut into
     1/2-inch slices
1   teaspoon minced shallots
2   tablespoons butter
1   cup chicken stock
     Salt and pepper to taste
1   pound tagliatelle, or other wide
     flat pasta
2   tablespoons butter
1/2 cup grated Parmigiano-
     Reggiano cheese

Grill the sausages until cooked through. Heat the olive oil in a large skillet over medium heat. Add the leeks and shallots; sauté for 5 minutes or until the leeks are tender. Add the sausages, 2 tablespoons butter and the stock to the skillet. Reduce the heat; simmer for 5 minutes. Season with salt and pepper. Meanwhile, cook the pasta according to the package directions; drain. Toss the pasta with 2 tablespoons butter, the leek sauce and the cheese. Serve immediately.

Makes 2 servings

Per serving
Calories 810 • Fat 34 g • Cholesterol 65 mg • Sodium 1380 mg • Carbohydrate 95 g • Fiber 4 g • Protein 20 g

Rotisserie Turkey with Apple Brandy

TURKEY

1	(14-pound) turkey
	Turkey Stock (below)
4	apples, quartered
2	large onions, quartered
1/4	cup (1/2 stick) butter, softened
2	tablespoons seasoned salt
1/2	cup apple brandy
1/2	cup (1/2 stick) butter

In 1886 a Mesa County exhibit of fruit was organized for the Denver Exposition.

—Mesa County Colorado: A 100-Year History

TURKEY STOCK

	Turkey giblets and neck
2	quarts water
2	onions, quartered
2	carrots, cut into chunks
2	to 3 ribs celery (with leaves), cut into chunks
1	tablespoon seasoned salt
1	teaspoon white pepper

For the turkey, remove the neck and giblets and reserve for the Turkey Stock. Rinse the turkey and pat dry. Fill the neck and body cavities with the apples and onions. Mix 1/4 cup butter and the seasoned salt until blended and rub all over the turkey. Pull the skin over the cavity openings and secure with skewers or kitchen string. Place the turkey on a rotisserie. Roast 3 3/4 to 4 1/2 hours or until a meat thermometer inserted into the thickest part of the thigh registers 180 to 185 degrees. Heat 4 cups of the turkey stock and add the brandy and 1/4 cup butter. Use this mixture to baste the bird every 20 to 30 minutes during cooking. Remove the turkey from the rotisserie; cover and let stand for 20 minutes before carving.

For the stock, combine the turkey giblets and neck, water, onions, carrots, celery, seasoned salt and white pepper in a stockpot or large saucepan. Bring to a boil; simmer for 15 minutes, skimming off the foam. Reduce the heat and simmer for several hours. Cool and strain the broth. Refrigerate, covered, until ready to use.

Makes 14 servings

Per serving

Calories 640 • Fat 30 g • Cholesterol 270 mg • Sodium 840 mg • Carbohydrate 11 g • Fiber 2 g • Protein 74 g

Grilled Chicken with Creamy Tequila Sauce

8   chicken breasts

2   limes

3/4   cup tequila

1/2   cup Triple Sec

2   cups vegetable oil

1 1/2   cups lime juice

2   tablespoons chopped fresh parsley

1   teaspoon chopped tarragon

1   garlic clove

1/2   cup finely chopped green bell pepper

1/2   cup finely chopped onion

    Salt and pepper to taste

2   to 3 pounds pasta of choice

1 1/2   cups milk

Arrange the chicken in a single layer in a nonreactive dish. Squeeze the juice from the limes into a bowl; chop the limes. Add the limes, tequila, Triple Sec, oil, 1 1/2 cups lime juice, parsley, tarragon, garlic, bell pepper, onion, salt and pepper to the freshly squeezed lime juice and mix well. Pour 2 cups of the mixture over the chicken, reserving the remainder. Marinate the chicken for 12 hours or longer, turning occasionally. Drain the chicken, discarding the used marinade. Grill the chicken over hot coals until juices run clear, turning once. Remove and keep warm. Cook the pasta using the package directions; drain. Heat the reserved marinade and the milk in a saucepan until hot. Divide the pasta evenly among 8 plates. Top each serving with chicken. Spoon the sauce over the top. Serve immediately. Note: You may substitute 32 peeled, deveined jumbo shrimp for the chicken.

Makes 8 servings

Per serving
Calories 1380 • Fat 63 g • Cholesterol 75 mg • Sodium 280 mg • Carbohydrate 138 g • Fiber 7 g • Protein 52 g

Mexican Chicken

1   baked or rotisserie chicken

1   (10-ounce) can cream of chicken soup

1   (10-ounce) can cream of
     mushroom soup

1   (4-ounce) can chopped green chiles

1   cup milk

1   tablespoon (or more) sour cream

1   tablespoon ground cumin

1   pound sharp Cheddar cheese,
     shredded

12   (6-inch) corn tortillas,
     torn into pieces

Remove the bones and skin from the chicken and cut the chicken into bite-size pieces. Combine the chicken soup, mushroom soup, green chiles, milk, sour cream and cumin in a large bowl and mix well. Fold in the chicken, 2 cups of the cheese and the tortillas. Spoon into a greased 9×13-inch baking dish. Bake at 350 degrees for 30 minutes or until bubbly. Top with the remaining 2 cups cheese. Bake for 10 minutes longer or until the cheese is melted. Let stand for 10 minutes before serving.

Makes 6 servings

From

Bennett's Bar-B-Que

Per serving

Calories 630 • Fat 37 g • Cholesterol 110 mg • Sodium 1350 mg • Carbohydrate 42 g • Fiber 2 g • Protein 29 g

Chicken Hot & Sweet

1/2 cup (1 stick) butter

1 cup orange juice

1/2 cup red currant jelly

1/4 cup Worcestershire sauce

1 tablespoon Dijon mustard

1 large garlic clove, minced

1 teaspoon ground ginger

3 dashes of Tabasco sauce

1 (3-pound) chicken, cut up

Combine the butter, orange juice, jelly, Worcestershire sauce, Dijon mustard, garlic, ginger and Tabasco sauce in a saucepan. Heat until the jelly is melted, stirring frequently. Cool. Arrange the chicken in a greased 9×13-inch baking dish. Pour the sauce over the chicken. Marinate, covered, in the refrigerator for 2 to 3 hours. Bake, uncovered, at 400 degrees for 1 hour or until the chicken is tender, dark brown and cooked through, basting frequently with the pan juices. Serve with rice.

Makes 4 servings

Sponsored By

The Horse in Sport

Per serving

Calories 510 • Fat 28 g • Cholesterol 135 mg • Sodium 515 mg • Carbohydrate 36 g • Fiber < 1 g • Protein 28 g

Chicken Tarragon

1	(3-pound) chicken, cut up
2	teaspoons salt
1/4	teaspoon pepper
	Dash of paprika
1/4	cup (1/2 stick) butter
1	onion, thinly sliced
1/2	cup canned sliced mushrooms, drained
1	teaspoon dried tarragon, crushed
1/4	cup water

Season the chicken with the salt, pepper and paprika. Melt the butter in a large skillet over medium heat and add the chicken. Cook until browned on all sides, turning occasionally. Remove the chicken from the skillet. Sauté the onion in the same skillet until tender and push to the side of the skillet. Return the chicken to the skillet. Add the mushrooms and tarragon; spoon the onion over the chicken. Add the water. Simmer, covered, for 30 to 40 minutes or until the chicken is tender and the juices run clear.

Makes 4 servings

A Grand Junction Dance Rink opened by the 1890s where the Mesa Theater is presently located.

—Mesa County Colorado: A 100-Year History

Per serving

Calories 550 • Fat 42 g • Cholesterol 205 mg • Sodium 970 mg • Carbohydrate 3 g • Fiber 1 g • Protein 36 g

Colorful Chicken Casserole

1 cup chopped celery

1 cup chopped green bell pepper

3/4 cup chopped onion

2 tablespoons butter

1 cup chicken broth

1 cup frozen corn kernels

1 cup frozen green peas

1 teaspoon salt

1/4 teaspoon pepper

3 cups cubed cooked chicken

7 to 8 ounces spaghetti, cooked and drained

1 (4-ounce) jar sliced mushrooms, drained

1 to 2 cups (4 to 8 ounces) shredded Cheddar cheese

Sauté the celery, bell pepper and onion in the butter in a large skillet until tender. Add the broth, corn kernels, peas, salt and pepper; cook until heated through. Stir in the chicken and spaghetti. Divide the mixture between two 8×8-inch greased baking dishes (or use a 9×13-inch baking dish for the entire mixture). Top with the mushrooms and cheese. Wrap 1 casserole tightly and freeze for future use. Bake 1 casserole, covered, at 350 degrees for 20 to 30 minutes. Uncover and bake 15 minutes longer. Note: Bake the frozen casserole, covered, at 350 degrees for 35 minutes. Uncover and bake for 15 minutes longer or until heated through.

Makes 8 servings

Per serving

Calories 360 • Fat 16 g • Cholesterol 65 mg • Sodium 1040 mg • Carbohydrate 32 g • Fiber 5 g • Protein 22 g

Chicken Broccoli Amandine Quiche

1 to 1 1/2 cups cubed cooked chicken

1 cup chopped cooked broccoli

1 cup (4 ounces) shredded Swiss cheese

1/4 cup grated Parmesan cheese

1 tablespoon chopped onion

1/2 teaspoon salt

1/8 teaspoon white pepper

1/2 cup sliced almonds, toasted

1 unbaked (9-inch) pie shell

4 eggs

1 cup milk

1/4 cup all-purpose flour

2 tablespoons fat-free sour cream

Combine the chicken, broccoli, Swiss cheese, Parmesan cheese, onion, salt, white pepper and 1/4 cup of the almonds in a large bowl; spoon into the pie shell. Whisk the eggs in a medium bowl. Whisk in the milk, flour and sour cream until blended. Pour the egg mixture over the filling. Sprinkle with the remaining 1/4 cup almonds. Bake at 350 degrees for 45 to 50 minutes or until the center is set. Cool for 10 minutes before cutting.

Makes 6 servings

Sponsored By

Doodles Bistro

Per serving
Calories 270 • Fat 16 g • Cholesterol 180 mg • Sodium 670 mg • Carbohydrate 12 g • Fiber 1 g • Protein 20 g

Macadamia Nut-Encrusted Halibut with Sun-Dried Tomato Cream Sauce

4   (6-ounce) halibut fillets or steaks

1   egg, beaten

2   cups finely chopped macadamia nuts

2   cups white wine

2   shallots, chopped

1/4 cup oil-pack sun-dried tomatoes, chopped

1   cup heavy cream

2   tablespoons cold butter

6   tablespoons butter

Dip the halibut in the egg and coat with the nuts. Wrap each fillet in plastic wrap and refrigerate for 1 hour. Combine the wine, shallots and sun-dried tomatoes in a saucepan; bring to a boil. Reduce the heat and simmer until nearly all the liquid has evaporated. Add the cream; simmer until reduced to about 1 cup. Stir in 2 tablespoons butter until melted. Melt 6 tablespoons butter in a large skillet; panfry each halibut fillet for 5 to 10 minutes or until the fish is golden brown and flakes easily with a fork. Serve the sauce over the halibut.

Makes 4 servings

For the fisherman, Western Colorado is a virtual paradise. The stream fishing is among the best in the world.

—A Land Alone: Colorado's Western Slope

Per serving

Calories 1140 • Fat 93 g • Cholesterol 210 mg • Sodium 340 mg • Carbohydrate 17 g • Fiber 6 g • Protein 48 g

Tuna with Wasabi Cream

Basques donned costumes for an international pageant during Grand Junction's seventy-fifth anniversary celebration. Mesa County's diverse ethnic groups also include Germans from Russia, Italians, Mexicans, Chinese, Japanese, and Indochinese refugees.

—Mesa County Colorado: A 100-Year History

2	teaspoons sesame seeds, toasted
2	teaspoons wasabi powder (dried Japanese horseradish)
2	teaspoons cracked pepper
1	teaspoon garlic powder
1/4	teaspoon salt
3	(6-ounce) tuna steaks (about 3/4 inch thick)
1	tablespoon wasabi powder
1	tablespoon water
1/4	cup mayonnaise (may use low-fat)
1/4	cup sour cream (may use low-fat or fat-free)
1	tablespoon fresh lemon juice
1	tablespoon low-sodium soy sauce
2	tablespoons sliced green onions

Combine the sesame seeds, 2 teaspoons wasabi powder, pepper, garlic powder and salt in a small bowl and rub over the tuna, coating completely. Refrigerate, covered, for 30 minutes. Stir 1 tablespoon wasabi powder into the water in a small bowl until dissolved; let stand for 5 minutes. Stir in the mayonnaise, sour cream, lemon juice and soy sauce and mix well. Place the steaks on a grill rack coated with nonstick cooking spray. Grill over hot coals for 5 minutes per side. Remove the tuna to a serving platter. Top with the wasabi sauce and the green onions.

Makes 3 servings

Per serving

Calories 340 • Fat 21 g • Cholesterol 70 mg • Sodium 420 mg • Carbohydrate 4 g • Fiber 1 g • Protein 31 g

Akumal Shrimp

1 cup soft herb cheese (may use light)

1/4 cup freshly grated Parmesan cheese

2 large garlic cloves, chopped

1/4 teaspoon Old Bay seafood seasoning

12 jumbo shrimp, peeled and deveined
(1 pound)

12 slices thick-cut bacon, partially cooked
(1 pound)

Combine the herb cheese, Parmesan cheese, garlic and seafood seasoning in a small bowl and mix to a paste consistency. Butterfly the shrimp. Stuff each shrimp with the cheese mixture. Wrap a slice of bacon around each stuffed shrimp. Arrange on a rack in a broiler pan. Broil for 5 to 10 minutes or until the cheese is browned and the shrimp turn pink.

Makes 4 servings

Sponsored By

Meridian Land Title LLC

Per serving

Calories 780 • Fat 72 g • Cholesterol 170 mg • Sodium 1290 mg • Carbohydrate 5 g • Fiber 0 g • Protein 21 g

Grilled Shrimp Tacos

TACOS

1 1/2	pounds large shrimp, peeled and deveined
4	limes, quartered
3	tablespoons butter, melted
4	large garlic cloves, minced
8	(6-inch) corn tortillas
2	cups finely shredded cabbage (or packaged coleslaw mix)
	Green tomatillo salsa
	Sour Cream Sauce (below)
	Salsa Fresco (below)

SOUR CREAM SAUCE

1/2	cup sour cream
3	tablespoons milk
3	tablespoons mayonnaise
1/2	teaspoon ground cumin
1/4	to 1/2 teaspoon cayenne pepper, or to taste

SALSA FRESCO

1 1/2	cups chopped seeded tomatoes
1	ripe avocado, diced
1/2	cup chopped green onions
1/4	cup (or more) chopped fresh cilantro

For the tacos, skewer the shrimp with the limes. Combine the butter and garlic in a small bowl and brush on the shrimp, coating completely. Grill over hot coals for 4 minutes per side or until the shrimp turn pink and the limes are browned. Meanwhile, grill the tortillas for 30 seconds per side, or warm in a large oiled skillet. Squeeze the grilled limes over the shrimp. Place the shrimp in the tortillas. Top with the cabbage, green salsa, sour cream sauce and salsa fresco and roll up as for lettuce wraps.

For the sauce, whisk together the sour cream, milk, mayonnaise, cumin and cayenne pepper in a small bowl until blended. Refrigerate until ready to serve.

For the salsa, combine the tomatoes, avocado, green onions and cilantro in a bowl. Refrigerate until ready to serve.

Makes 8 servings

In 1882 the first school opened with Nannie Blain as schoolmarm.

—Mesa County Colorado: A 100-Year History

Per serving

Calories 290 • Fat 14 g • Cholesterol 155 mg • Sodium 230 mg • Carbohydrate 22 g • Fiber 2 g • Protein 20 g

Shrimp in Cream Sauce

1/2 large onion, chopped
6 to 8 tablespoons butter
1 (10-ounce) can diced tomatoes
    with green chiles
1 (10-ounce) can cream of
    mushroom soup
12 ounces peeled shrimp

Sauté the onion in 2 tablespoons of the butter in a large skillet or medium saucepan until tender. Add the remaining butter and heat until melted. Stir in the tomatoes with green chiles and the soup and bring to a boil. Reduce the heat to low and simmer for several minutes. Add the shrimp; cook for 3 to 5 minutes or until the shrimp turn pink, stirring occasionally. Serve with pasta or rice.

Makes 4 servings

Sponsored By

Patti Milius

Per serving

Calories 300 • Fat 22 g • Cholesterol 135 mg • Sodium 770 mg • Carbohydrate 10 g • Fiber 1 g • Protein 14 g

Shrimp Boil

Two men first saw the possibilities of the valley as a fruit-raising mecca. One was Elam Blain, who planted peach seeds between Grand Junction and Palisade near the Grand River in 1882. The other was William Pabor, who planted fruit trees near today's Fruita in 1883.

—A Land Alone: Colorado's Western Slope

4	quarts water
1/4	cup Old Bay seafood seasoning (or crab boil seasoning)
2	to 3 teaspoons cayenne pepper
2	pounds smoked sausage, cut into 1-inch chunks
2	pounds small new potatoes
10	small onions
5	ears of corn, shucked and cut in half crosswise
2	pounds large unpeeled shrimp
1/4	cup (1/2 stick) butter, melted
1/4	cup snipped fresh herbs, such as thyme, oregano and/or parsley

Combine the water, seafood seasoning and cayenne pepper in a 10-quart Dutch oven or large stockpot. Cover and bring to a boil. Add the sausage, potatoes, onions and corn and return to a boil. Reduce the heat; simmer, covered, for 10 minutes. Add the shrimp; cook, covered, for 2 to 3 minutes or until the shrimp turn pink. Remove from the heat and let stand for 5 minutes. Drain in a large colander and spoon into a large serving bowl. Drizzle with the butter and sprinkle with the herbs. Serve with cocktail sauce and hot red pepper sauce if desired.

Makes 10 servings

Per serving

Calories 530 • Fat 30 g • Cholesterol 225 mg • Sodium 1170 mg • Carbohydrate 31 g • Fiber 4 g • Protein 34 g

Spicy Shrimp & Nectarine Sauté

1/4 cup (1/2 stick) butter

4 teaspoons minced garlic

1/2 cup diced red bell pepper

1/2 cup diced green bell pepper

3 tablespoons finely chopped
green onions

3 tablespoons lemon juice

1 teaspoon dried thyme leaves

1 teaspoon coarsely ground black pepper

1 teaspoon cayenne pepper

1/2 teaspoon seasoned salt

1 tablespoon finely chopped fresh basil

24 large shrimp, peeled and deveined
(about 1 pound)

4 nectarines, thinly sliced

1 pound angel hair pasta, cooked
and drained

Melt the butter in a large skillet. Add the garlic, bell peppers, green onions, lemon juice, thyme, black pepper, cayenne pepper, seasoned salt and basil; sauté for 2 minutes. Add the shrimp and cook for about 3 minutes or until the shrimp start to turn pink, stirring occasionally. Add the nectarines; cook for 2 to 3 minutes longer or until the shrimp are pink (do not overcook). Serve immediately over the pasta. Garnish with lemon wedges and chopped parsley.

Makes 4 servings

From

Nero's Italian Restaurant

Per serving
Calories 650 • Fat 16 g • Cholesterol 95 mg • Sodium 330 mg • Carbohydrate 102 g • Fiber 7 g • Protein 26 g

Seafood Gumbo

ROUX

1/2	cup lard or shortening
1/2	cup all-purpose flour
1/2	cup chopped onion
1/4	cup chopped bell pepper
1/4	cup chopped celery

GUMBO

6	large tomatoes, or 2 (15-ounce) cans tomatoes
1	tablespoon shortening
1	whole chicken, cut into pieces
2	(1/2-inch-thick) ham slices, chopped
1	onion, chopped
1/2	pod red pepper, seeded and chopped
1	sprig each of parsley and thyme, chopped
1	can okra, rinsed, drained and chopped, or 1 (16-ounce) package frozen okra
3	quarts boiling water
1	bay leaf
	Salt and cayenne pepper to taste
1	teaspoon oregano
2	tablespoons Worcestershire sauce
1	pound medium shrimp
1	pound crab meat
2	cups rice, cooked

When small canneries in the Grand Valley contracted for tomatoes, many farmers turned part of their land into tomato fields.

—Mesa County Colorado: A 100-Year History

For the roux, heat the lard in a heavy skillet or saucepan. Add the flour gradually, stirring constantly until smooth. Reduce the heat and stir until of the desired color; do not burn. Remove from the heat and stir in the onion, bell pepper and celery.

For the gumbo, peel and chop the tomatoes, reserving the juice. Heat the shortening in a large soup kettle until hot. Add the chicken and ham. Simmer, covered, for 10 minutes. Stir in the tomatoes, onion, red pepper, parsley and thyme. Add the okra and cook until browned, stirring frequently. Stir in the reserved tomato juice. Pour in the water. Add the bay leaf, salt, cayenne pepper, oregano and Worcestershire sauce. Simmer for 1 hour, stirring occasionally. Add the shrimp and crab meat. Cook for 10 to 15 minutes. Serve over hot cooked rice. Note: To serve 12, use 2 chickens, 2 pounds of shrimp and 2 pounds of crab meat. You may leave the chicken on the bones and the shrimp and crab meat in the shell.

Makes 6 servings

Per serving

Calories 360 • Fat 7 g • Cholesterol 195 mg • Sodium 2160 mg • Carbohydrate 31 g • Fiber 4 g • Protein 44 g

Sour Cream Enchiladas

1	baked or rotisserie chicken
1/2	cup (or less) vegetable oil
12	(6-inch) corn tortillas
1	cup chopped onion
2	(4-ounce) cans chopped green chiles
1 1/2	cups sour cream
16	ounces mild Mexican Velveeta cheese, cut into cubes
1	(5-ounce) can evaporated milk

Remove the bones and skin from the chicken and cut the chicken into bite-size pieces. Heat the oil to medium-high in a small saucepan or skillet. Heat 1 tortilla at a time in the hot oil for 3 to 5 seconds per side. Repeat for all the tortillas. Place 3 to 5 tablespoons of the chicken in the center of each tortilla; top with 1 tablespoon onion, 2 teaspoons green chiles and 2 teaspoons sour cream. Roll up the tortilla and place seam side down in a 9×13-inch baking dish. Combine the cheese and milk in a large microwave-safe bowl. Microwave on High for 3 to 4 minutes or until the cheese is melted, stirring after each minute. Pour the cheese mixture over the enchiladas. Cover with foil. Bake at 350 degrees for 25 minutes. Serve with shredded lettuce, chopped tomatoes and salsa if desired.

Makes 4 servings

Per serving
Calories 1800 • Fat 112 g • Cholesterol 425 mg • Sodium 1970 mg • Carbohydrate 66 g • Fiber 4 g • Protein 123 g

Portobello Pasta Milano

1/2 cup sliced black olives

1/2 cup chopped sun-dried tomatoes

2 garlic cloves, minced

2 tablespoons olive oil

1/2 cup chopped portobello mushrooms

1/2 cup white wine

1 teaspoon basil

4 cups fresh baby greens

1/2 to 1 pound linguini, cooked and drained

1/4 cup pine nuts, toasted

1/4 cup grated Parmesan cheese

1 tablespoon chopped fresh parsley

Sauté the olives, sun-dried tomatoes and garlic in 1 tablespoon of the olive oil in a small saucepan. Sauté the mushrooms in the remaining 1 tablespoon olive oil in another small saucepan or skillet. Add 1/2 of the wine to each saucepan, stirring to deglaze the pans. Add the basil to the tomato mixture. Bring the tomato mixture to a boil and simmer until the wine is reduced by 1/2. Place the greens on top of the tomato mixture; cover and steam. Place the linguini in a serving bowl and top with the greens and tomato mixture. Top with the mushrooms. Sprinkle with the pine nuts, cheese and parsley.

Makes 4 servings

From

Rockslide Brewery

Per serving

Calories 430 • Fat 18 g • Cholesterol 5 mg • Sodium 250 mg • Carbohydrate 52 g • Fiber 5 g • Protein 12 g

Spinach Baked with Feta

3 tablespoons extra-virgin olive oil

1 small onion, finely chopped

2 pounds spinach

Nutmeg for grating

Sea salt or kosher salt to taste

Freshly ground pepper to taste

3/4 cup (6 ounces) crumbled feta cheese

3/4 cup ricotta cheese, drained for at least 1 hour

1/2 cup coarsely chopped flat-leaf parsley

1 to 2 tablespoons extra-virgin olive oil

Combine 3 tablespoons olive oil and the onion in a large skillet. Cook over low heat for 15 to 20 minutes or until the onion is tender, stirring occasionally. Stir in the spinach. Grate about 1/2 teaspoon nutmeg over the spinach. Season with salt and pepper. Cook for 5 minutes. Remove from the heat and pour off any liquid. Stir in the feta cheese, ricotta cheese and parsley. Spoon the mixture into an oiled gratin dish or other small shallow baking dish. Drizzle with 1 to 2 tablespoons olive oil. Bake at 350 degrees for 20 minutes. Cool to room temperature before serving.

Makes 4 servings

Per serving

Calories 360 • Fat 28 g • Cholesterol 30 mg • Sodium 750 mg • Carbohydrate 15 g • Fiber 7 g • Protein 16 g

Savory Vegetable Pie

Grand Junction became the name for the settlement at the Grand (later Colorado) and Gunnison rivers in November 1881. In part, the name derives from its location at the juncture of two great tides of immigration, one from the East, the other from the West.

—Charles McCormick collection

CROUTON CRUST

2	cups garlic and onion croutons, crushed
1/4	cup (1/2 stick) butter, melted

VEGETABLE FILLING

1	cup chopped onion
1	garlic clove, minced
1/4	cup (1/2 stick) butter
1	head cauliflower or broccoli, chopped (about 3 cups)
1/2	cup chopped carrots
1/2	teaspoon dried savory or thyme
1/4	teaspoon dried oregano
	Salt and pepper to taste
1 1/2	cups (6 ounces) shredded Cheddar cheese
2	eggs
1/4	cup milk

For the crust, combine the crushed croutons and butter in a small bowl and mix well. Press into a 9-inch pie plate and set aside.

For the filling, sauté the onion and garlic in the butter in a large skillet. Add the cauliflower, carrots, savory, oregano, salt and pepper. Cook, covered, for 10 minutes. Sprinkle 3/4 cup of the cheese over the crust. Add the vegetable mixture and top with the remaining 3/4 cup cheese. Whisk together the eggs and milk in a small bowl and pour over the filling. Bake at 375 degrees for 35 minutes. Let stand for 10 minutes before cutting.

Makes 8 servings

Per serving
Calories 370 • Fat 25 g • Cholesterol 105 mg • Sodium 870 mg • Carbohydrate 28 g • Fiber 3 g • Protein 13 g

Vegetarian Chili

1/3 cup chopped green bell pepper

1/3 cup chopped onion

1 rib celery, chopped

1/2 cup vegetable oil

1 (28-ounce) can whole tomatoes

1 (15-ounce) can cut green beans, drained

1 (15-ounce) can kidney beans, drained

1 (15-ounce) can peas, drained

2 to 4 teaspoons chili powder, or to taste

2 teaspoons salt

1 large garlic clove, minced

1/2 teaspoon seasoned salt

1/8 teaspoon MSG (optional)

Cook the bell pepper, onion and celery in the oil in a large saucepan over medium-low heat for 30 minutes or until tender, stirring occasionally. Add the tomatoes, green beans, kidney beans, peas, chili powder, salt, garlic, seasoned salt and MSG. Bring to a boil; reduce the heat and simmer for 15 minutes, stirring occasionally. Note: For Chicken Chili, add 1 to 2 cups cubed cooked chicken.

Makes 8 servings

Sponsored By

Ron Jens

Coldwell Banker

Per serving

Calories 240 • Fat 14 g • Cholesterol 0 mg • Sodium 1180 mg • Carbohydrate 23 g • Fiber 6 g • Protein 7 g

Winter

Desserts & Drinks

Winter Menu

Cranberry Cream Cheese Appetizer

Charlemagne Salad

Filet Mignon with Shiitake Mushroom Sauce

Asparagus Bundles

Rosemary Reds

Christmas Pie

Italian Cream Cake

CAKE

1/2	cup light butter, softened
2	cups sugar
2	egg yolks
2	cups all-purpose flour
1	teaspoon baking soda
1	cup buttermilk
1/2	cup chopped pecans
1	teaspoon butter extract
1	teaspoon coconut extract
1	teaspoon vanilla extract
6	egg whites, at room temperature
	Cream Cheese Frosting (below)

For the cake, coat the bottoms (not sides) of three 9-inch cake pans with nonstick cooking spray and line with waxed paper. Coat the waxed paper with nonstick cooking spray and dust with flour. Beat the butter at medium speed in a large mixing bowl until creamy. Beat in the sugar gradually until well blended. Beat in the egg yolks 1 at a time. Stir together the flour and baking soda. Add the flour mixture to the butter mixture alternately with the buttermilk, mixing well after each addition. Stir in the pecans and extracts. Beat the egg whites in a mixing bowl until stiff peaks form; fold into the batter. Pour the batter into the prepared pans. Bake at 350 degrees for 20 to 23 minutes or until the layers test done. Cool in the pans for 10 minutes. Remove the layers to a wire rack to cool completely. Spread the frosting between the layers and over the top and side of the cake. Garnish with lemon peel strips.

CREAM CHEESE FROSTING

8	ounces Neufchâtel cheese, softened
1	tablespoon light butter, softened
1	(1-pound) package confectioners' sugar
1	teaspoon vanilla extract

For the frosting, combine the cheese, butter and sugar in a large mixing bowl and beat until smooth. Stir in the vanilla. Refrigerate, covered, until well chilled.

Makes 10 servings

Per serving

Calories 840 • Fat 22 g • Cholesterol 95 mg • Sodium 430 mg • Carbohydrate 153 g • Fiber 1 g • Protein 12 g

Rum Cake

CAKE

1   (18-ounce) package yellow cake mix
1   (4-ounce) package vanilla instant pudding mix
4   eggs
1/2 cup water
1/2 cup vegetable oil
1/2 cup light rum
1   cup chopped pecans
     Rum Glaze (below)

RUM GLAZE

1/2 cup (1 stick) butter
1/2 cup sugar
1/4 to 1/2 cup light rum
1/4 cup water

For the cake, combine the cake mix, pudding mix, eggs, water, oil and rum in a bowl and mix well. Sprinkle the pecans onto the bottom of a greased and floured bundt pan. Pour the batter into the pan. Bake at 350 degrees for 35 to 45 minutes or until the cake tests done. Cool in the pan for 15 minutes. Invert the cake onto a serving plate. Poke holes in the cake with a bamboo skewer. Pour the warm glaze slowly over the cake.

For the glaze, combine the butter, sugar, rum and water in a small saucepan and heat until the butter is melted and the sugar is dissolved, stirring frequently.

Makes 12 servings

Per serving
Calories 570 • Fat 31 g • Cholesterol 90 mg • Sodium 490 mg • Carbohydrate 58 g • Fiber 1 g • Protein 5 g

Becky's Chocolate Cake

CHOCOLATE CAKE

2	cups all-purpose flour
2	cups sugar
1	teaspoon baking soda
1/2	cup (1 stick) butter
1/4	cup baking cocoa
1	cup water
1/2	cup vegetable oil
1/2	cup buttermilk
2	eggs, beaten
1	teaspoon vanilla extract
	Chocolate Glaze (below)

CHOCOLATE GLAZE

3	ounces semisweet chocolate
6	tablespoons butter
2	cups confectioners' sugar
1	teaspoon vanilla extract
	Water

For the cake, stir together the flour, sugar and baking soda in a large mixing bowl. Combine the butter, baking cocoa, water and oil in a saucepan; bring to a boil. Pour over the flour mixture and beat for 2 minutes. Beat in the buttermilk and eggs until blended. Stir in the vanilla. Pour the batter into a greased and floured bundt pan. Bake at 350 degrees for 50 to 55 minutes or until the cake tests done. Cool in the pan for 15 minutes. Invert onto a serving plate and cool completely. Drizzle the chocolate glaze over the cake.

For the glaze, melt the chocolate and butter in a small saucepan over low heat, stirring constantly. Pour the chocolate mixture into a medium bowl. Whisk the confectioners' sugar and vanilla into the chocolate until well blended. Whisk in water, 1 tablespoon at a time, until the glaze is the consistency of a thin batter.

Makes 12 servings

From

Blue Moon

Per serving

Calories 500 • Fat 27 g • Cholesterol 70 mg • Sodium 230 mg • Carbohydrate 62 g • Fiber 2 g • Protein 4 g

Chocolate & Strawberry Cake

1 1/2 cups all-purpose flour

1 cup sugar

3 tablespoons baking cocoa

1 teaspoon baking soda

1/8 teaspoon salt

5 tablespoons vegetable oil

1 teaspoon vanilla extract

1 teaspoon vinegar

1 cup cold water

1 cup chopped strawberries

Stir together the flour, sugar, baking cocoa, baking soda and salt in a large bowl. Make 3 holes in the flour mixture. Pour the oil into the first hole, the vanilla into the second and the vinegar into the third. Pour the water over the top and mix well with a wooden spoon. Stir in the strawberries. Pour the batter into a greased 8×8-inch cake pan. Bake at 350 degrees for 30 to 35 minutes or until the cake tests done. Cool in the pan for 10 minutes before cutting. Dust with confectioners' sugar and serve with additional strawberries if desired.

Makes 8 servings

Sponsored By

Bob and Shirley Jess

Custom Music

Per serving
Calories 265 • Fat 9.5 g • Cholesterol 0 mg • Sodium 195 mg • Carbohydrate 45 g • Fiber 2 g • Protein 3 g

Strawberry Jam Cake

1	tablespoon vinegar
1	cup sour milk
1	cup (2 sticks) margarine, softened
1¹/2	cups sugar
4	eggs
1	cup strawberry jam
1	cup chopped dates
1	cup chopped pecans
3	cups all-purpose flour
1	teaspoon baking soda
1	teaspoon ground cinnamon
¹/2	teaspoon salt
1	teaspoon vanilla extract

Stir the vinegar into the milk and let stand for 10 minutes (or use buttermilk). Cream the margarine and sugar in a large mixing bowl until light and fluffy. Beat in the eggs 1 at a time. Add the jam, dates, pecans and the milk mixture and mix well. Sift together the flour, baking soda, cinnamon and salt; add to the batter and mix well. Stir in the vanilla. Pour into 2 greased and floured loaf pans. Bake at 350 degrees for 45 to 60 minutes or until the loaves test done. Cool in the pans for 15 minutes. Invert onto serving plates and cool completely.

Makes 10 servings

Per serving

Calories 630 • Fat 27 g • Cholesterol 0 mg • Sodium 470 mg • Carbohydrate 95 g • Fiber 4 g • Protein 7 g

Swedish Nut Cake

CAKE

2   eggs

2   cups sugar

2   cups all-purpose flour

1/2   cup chopped walnuts

2   teaspoons baking soda

1   (20-ounce) can juice-pack crushed pineapple

1   tablespoon vanilla extract
     Cream Cheese Icing (below)

CREAM CHEESE ICING

8   ounces cream cheese, softened

1/2   cup (1 stick) butter or margarine, softened

13/4 cups confectioners' sugar

1/2   cup chopped walnuts

1   teaspoon vanilla extract

For the cake, combine the eggs, sugar, flour, walnuts, baking soda, pineapple and vanilla in a large mixing bowl and mix well. Pour the batter into a 9×13-inch cake pan coated with nonstick cooking spray. Bake at 350 degrees for 35 to 45 minutes or until the cake tests done. Cool in the pan just until warm (the cake may fall a little in the center). Spread the icing over the warm cake.

For the icing, combine the cream cheese and butter in a large mixing bowl and beat until fluffy. Add the confectioners' sugar and beat until smooth. Stir in the walnuts and vanilla.

Makes 16 servings

Per serving

Calories 340 • Fat 12 g • Cholesterol 25 mg • Sodium 210 mg • Carbohydrate 56 g • Fiber 1 g • Protein 3 g

Peaches and Cream

1 cup heavy whipping cream

1/4 cup granulated sugar

16 ounces cream cheese, softened

3/4 cup confectioners' sugar

1 cup frozen sweetened raspberries, thawed

1 tablespoon cornstarch

2 (or more) ripe Palisade peaches, peeled

Combine the whipping cream and granulated sugar in a chilled deep mixing bowl and beat until stiff. Combine the cream cheese and confectioners' sugar in a large mixing bowl and beat until light and fluffy. Fold in the whipped cream. Spoon or pipe the cream mixture into individual serving dishes. Refrigerate for 2 hours or until chilled. Press and strain the raspberries through a sieve, reserving the juice; discard the pulp and seeds. Add water to the raspberry juice to equal 1 cup. Pour the juice into a saucepan. Stir in the cornstarch until blended. Cook until thickened, stirring constantly. Cool. Chop or slice the peaches and spoon over the cream mixture. Drizzle the raspberry sauce over the top.

This recipe was a contest winner at the Palisade Peach Festival.

Makes 8 servings

Sponsored By

Arlene and Dennis Baker

Palisade was laid out in 1893 east of Grand Junction and became the center of the peach industry in Colorado. . . . A breeze called the "peach wind" blew down the canyon at night, protecting the upper valley from frost. In season, more than two hundred refrigerated railroad cars of peaches per day were shipped from the Grand Valley, with ninety percent coming from Palisade.

—A Land Alone: Colorado's Western Slope

Per serving
Calories 440 • Fat 31 g • Cholesterol 105 mg • Sodium 180 mg • Carbohydrate 39 g • Fiber 1 g • Protein 5 g

Fresh Peach Dessert

CRUST

1 1/4	cups all-purpose flour
1/2	cup extra-light olive oil
1/3	cup finely chopped pecans
3	tablespoons sugar
2	tablespoons heavy cream
3/4	teaspoon salt

FILLING AND ASSEMBLY

60	large marshmallows (about 16 ounces)
1/2	cup milk
8	ounces cream cheese, softened
2	cups frozen nondairy whipped topping, thawed
	Ripe Palisade peaches, peeled and sliced
	Orange Glaze (below)

ORANGE GLAZE

2 1/2	cups water
3/4	cup sugar
1	tablespoon fresh lemon juice
2	tablespoons cornstarch
2	tablespoons cold water
1	(3-ounce) package orange gelatin

Palisade peaches have won many prizes in national and international shows.

—Mesa County Colorado: A 100-Year History

For the crust, combine the flour, olive oil, pecans, sugar, cream and salt in a bowl and mix well. Press into a 9×13-inch baking pan. Bake at 400 degrees for 15 to 18 minutes. Set aside to cool completely.

For the filling and assembly, melt the marshmallows with the milk in a large heavy saucepan over low heat, stirring occasionally. Stir in the cream cheese until well blended. Cool completely. Fold in the whipped topping. Spread over the crust. Chill until set. Arrange the peaches over the marshmallow filling. Spoon the glaze over the peaches and refrigerate until set.

For the glaze, combine 2 1/2 cups water, the sugar and lemon juice in a saucepan and bring to a boil. Combine the cornstarch and 2 tablespoons water in a small bowl, stirring until blended. Add the cornstarch mixture and the gelatin to the saucepan. Cook until the gelatin is dissolved and the mixture has thickened, stirring constantly. Cool.

Makes 12 servings

Per serving

Calories 490 • Fat 23 g • Cholesterol 25 mg • Sodium 230 mg • Carbohydrate 70 g • Fiber 1 g • Protein 4 g

Pavlova with Strawberry Cream

PAVLOVA

4   egg whites, at room temperature
1   cup sugar
1   teaspoon vanilla extract
     Strawberry Cream (below)
     Sliced strawberries

For the pavlova, line a 9×13-inch baking pan with parchment paper, extending the paper 2 inches over the sides of the pan. Place the egg whites in a large mixing bowl and beat at high speed until soft peaks form. Add the sugar gradually, beating until the sugar is dissolved and stiff peaks form. Add the vanilla and beat for 1 minute. Spread in the prepared pan. Bake at 350 degrees for 30 to 40 minutes. Remove from the oven and cool in the pan for 5 minutes. Invert onto a platter and peel off the parchment paper. Place the pavlova top side up on the a serving platter. Cool completely. Spread the strawberry cream on top and garnish with the sliced strawberries. Note: Kiwifruit or other fresh fruit can be used instead of strawberries.

STRAWBERRY CREAM

1 1/2 cups heavy whipping cream
1/4   cup sugar
2   cups chopped strawberries
1/4   cup Cointreau, brandy, rum or orange juice (optional), or 1 teaspoon vanilla extract (optional)

For the strawberry cream, combine the cream and sugar in a chilled deep mixing bowl and beat until stiff. Fold in the berries and liqueur. Refrigerate until ready to use.

Makes 12 servings

In 1923 Palisade established the United Fruit Growers. This cooperative organization still serves the area.

—Mesa County Colorado: A 100-Year History

Per serving
Calories 240 • Fat 13.5 g • Cholesterol 50 mg • Sodium 35 mg • Carbohydrate 28 g • Fiber 1 g • Protein 2 g

Enstrom's Almond Toffee Cheesecake

3 1/2 cups crushed vanilla wafers

1/4 cup (1/2 stick) butter, melted

16 ounces cream cheese, softened

2 cups sugar

5 teaspoons all-purpose flour

1 tablespoon ground cinnamon

6 eggs

2 egg yolks

3/4 cup sour cream

3/4 cup heavy cream

1 1/2 teaspoons almond extract

1 1/2 teaspoons vanilla extract

12 ounces Enstrom's Almond Toffee, coarsely crushed

Mix the vanilla wafer crumbs and butter in a bowl. Press onto the bottom of a greased 9-inch springform pan. Bake at 350 degrees for 10 minutes or until lightly browned. Remove from the oven and cool. Press heavy-duty foil tightly over the bottom and side of the pan. Combine the cream cheese, sugar, flour and cinnamon in a large mixing bowl; beat until light and fluffy. Beat in the eggs and egg yolks 1 at a time. Beat in the sour cream, heavy cream and extracts at low speed until well blended. Fold about 1/2 cup of the crushed toffee into the batter. Pour the batter into the prepared crust. Set the pan into a larger shallow pan of hot water. Top the cheesecake with the remaining toffee. Bake in the water bath at 350 degrees for 1 hour and 20 minutes or until the edge springs back when lightly touched (the center will be slightly soft). Cool completely before removing the side of the pan. Chill.

Makes 8 servings

From

Enstrom's Candies

Per serving

Calories 480 • Fat 32 g • Cholesterol 190 mg • Sodium 250 mg • Carbohydrate 42 g • Fiber 1 g • Protein 7 g

The Creamiest New York Cheesecake Ever

24 ounces cream cheese, softened
4 eggs
2 cups sour cream
1 cup heavy cream
1 cup sugar
1/2 cup (1 stick) unsalted butter, melted
2 tablespoons all-purpose flour
2 teaspoons vanilla extract
1 teaspoon lemon juice

Press heavy-duty foil tightly over the bottom and side of a 10-inch springform pan. Combine the cream cheese, eggs, sour cream, heavy cream, sugar, butter, flour, vanilla and lemon juice in a large mixing bowl. Beat at low speed for 10 to 15 minutes or until smooth and fluffy. Pour into the prepared pan. Set the pan into a larger shallow pan of hot water. Bake in the water bath at 325 degrees for 20 minutes. Reduce the oven temperature to 300 degrees and bake for 40 minutes longer. Turn off the oven; leave the cheesecake in the oven for 1 hour (do not open the oven door). Cool completely before removing side of the pan. Chill. Garnish with whipped cream and serve with fresh fruit if desired.

Makes 10 servings

Sponsored By
Comfort Air of Grand Junction

Per serving
Calories 610 • Fat 52 g • Cholesterol 245 mg • Sodium 280 mg • Carbohydrate 26 g • Fiber 0 g • Protein 10 g

Custard Baked in Phyllo

CUSTARD

8	cups milk
6	egg whites, at room temperature
1 1/2	cups sugar
6	egg yolks
1	cup farina (or Cream of Wheat)
1	cup (2 sticks) unsalted butter, melted
1	pound frozen phyllo pastry, thawed (See Note page 129) Honey Syrup (page 129)
1 1/2	teaspoons vanilla extract

For the custard, pour the milk into a large heavy saucepan and bring to a boil; remove from the heat. Place the egg whites in a large mixing bowl and beat until stiff peaks form. Beat in the sugar and egg yolks until smooth and well blended. Stir in the farina gradually and mix well. Stir in the hot milk gradually. Return the mixture to the saucepan; cook over low heat until thickened, stirring constantly. Remove from the heat and continue stirring until the mixture cools. Stir in the vanilla. Brush a 9×13-inch baking pan with melted butter. Brush each phyllo sheet generously with butter. Place half the buttered phyllo in the bottom of the pan with the edges extending over the sides of the pan. Spread the custard mixture evenly in the phyllo-lined pan. Fold the edges of the phyllo over the custard. Place the remaining phyllo sheets over the custard, brushing each with butter. Score the surface of the pastry with a sharp knife into 5 strips lengthwise and about 2 1/2 inches in width, cutting through only the top layer. Bake at 350 degrees for 45 minutes or until the custard is firm and the top is golden brown. Carefully spoon the honey syrup over the entire top. Cool completely before cutting.

Makes 12 servings

HONEY SYRUP

1 1/2 cups water

2 cups sugar

1/2 cup honey

1/2 teaspoon lemon juice

1/4 cup brandy

1 teaspoon grated lemon zest

For the syrup, combine the water, sugar, honey and lemon juice in a saucepan and bring to a boil. Simmer over low heat for 15 minutes. Remove from the heat and stir in the brandy and lemon zest. Cool. Note: Thaw phyllo dough, unopened, in the refrigerator overnight. It dries out quickly, so do not open the package until the filling has been prepared. Unroll the phyllo and cover with waxed paper topped with a damp towel. Keep the unused portions covered until needed. This dessert is best made a day ahead so the syrup absorbs. Refrigerate, covered, for up to 2 days.

Per serving
Calories 770 • Fat 31 g • Cholesterol 155 mg • Sodium 250 mg • Carbohydrate 109 g • Fiber 3 g • Protein 13 g

Old-Fashioned Bread Pudding

4 eggs

1/2 cup sugar

2 cups heavy cream

1/4 teaspoon ground cinnamon

Pinch of salt

2 cups (1/2-inch) bread cubes (French bread or challah)

Whisk the eggs in a medium bowl. Whisk in the sugar, cream, cinnamon and salt until well blended. Place the bread cubes in a buttered 1-quart soufflé dish. Pour the cream mixture over the bread. Bake at 375 degrees for 45 minutes or until browned. Serve warm with cream and fresh fruit if desired.

Makes 6 servings

Per serving
Calories 420 • Fat 33 g • Cholesterol 250 mg • Sodium 210 mg • Carbohydrate 25 g • Fiber 0 g • Protein 7 g

Christmas Cranberry Pudding with Butter Sauce

PUDDING

1 1/3 cups all-purpose flour
1 teaspoon baking soda
1/2 teaspoon salt
1/2 cup dark molasses
1/2 cup boiling water
2 cups fresh cranberries
Butter Sauce (below)

BUTTER SAUCE

1/2 cup (1 stick) butter
1 cup sugar
1/2 cup evaporated milk

For the pudding, stir together the flour, baking soda and salt in a bowl. Add the molasses and water and mix well. Stir in the cranberries. Pour the batter into a buttered 1-pound coffee can. Cover tightly with a double layer of foil; tie securely with string. Place the can on a rack in a large kettle. Add boiling water to reach halfway up the can. Steam for 2 hours. Serve with Butter Sauce. Note: Double all ingredients to fill a 2-pound coffee can and steam for 3 hours.

For the sauce, combine the butter, sugar and evaporated milk in a saucepan. Cook until the butter and sugar are melted and the mixture is smooth, stirring frequently.

Makes 8 servings

Sponsored By

Patti Chamberlain and Bob Fisher

Per serving
Calories 270 • Fat 13 g • Cholesterol 35 mg • Sodium 200 mg • Carbohydrate 39 g • Fiber 1 g • Protein 1 g

S'more Pizza Please!

1/4 cup chocolate hazelnut spread (such as Nutella)

1 refrigerator pizza crust

2 cups semisweet chocolate chips

6 graham crackers, coarsely crushed

2 1/2 cups miniature marshmallows

Spread the chocolate hazelnut spread over the crust, covering completely. Sprinkle with the chocolate chips. Place the crust on a pizza pan or baking sheet. Bake at 375 degrees for 3 minutes or until the chocolate chips are melted. Top with the graham crackers and marshmallows. Bake for 8 minutes longer or until the marshmallows are puffed and browned.

Makes 12 servings

From

Pablo's Pizza

Per serving

Calories 340 • Fat 12 g • Cholesterol 0 mg • Sodium 240 mg • Carbohydrate 56 g • Fiber 1 g • Protein 3 g

Yum-Yum Salad

1 (4-ounce) package cheesecake instant pudding mix
1 cup buttermilk
8 ounces cream cheese, softened
1 (8-ounce) container frozen nondairy whipped topping, thawed
1/2 pint raspberries
1/2 pint blueberries
1 pint (3/4 pound) strawberries, halved
2 cups seedless green grapes
2 cups seedless red grapes
1 (8-ounce) can mandarin oranges, drained
1 (8-ounce) can pineapple tidbits, drained
2 to 3 Palisade peaches, peeled and sliced

Combine the pudding mix and the buttermilk in a small mixing bowl. Beat for 2 minutes or until smooth. Beat the cream cheese in a large mixing bowl until fluffy. Stir in the pudding until blended. Fold in the whipped topping. Fold in the raspberries, blueberries, strawberries, green and red grapes, mandarin oranges and pineapple. Spoon into a large serving bowl and chill. Top with the sliced peaches to serve.

Makes 12 servings

The fruit crop in 1911, the year of the greatest yield, passed the million dollar mark.

—Mesa County Colorado: A 100-Year History

Per serving
Calories 210 • Fat 11 g • Cholesterol 20 mg • Sodium 90 mg • Carbohydrate 27 g • Fiber 2 g • Protein 3 g

Colorado Apple Pie

6   large tart apples, peeled and sliced

1   unbaked (9- or 10-inch) pie shell

3/4   cup gingersnap crumbs

1/3   to 1/2 cup sugar

1/4   cup (1/2 stick) butter, softened

1   tablespoon all-purpose flour

1/2   teaspoon ground cinnamon

   Pinch of salt

1/4   cup chopped walnuts

1/3   cup maple syrup

Place half the apples in the pie shell. Mix the gingersnap crumbs, sugar, butter, flour, cinnamon and salt in a bowl. Sprinkle half the crumb mixture over the apples. Top with the remaining apples. Sprinkle with the remaining crumb mixture and the walnuts. Bake at 375 degrees for 50 minutes, covering with foil during the last 10 minutes. Remove from the oven and pour the syrup over the pie. Cool for 10 minutes before slicing.

Makes 8 servings

Per serving

Calories 320 • Fat 12 g • Cholesterol 15 mg • Sodium 150 mg • Carbohydrate 51 g • Fiber 3 g • Protein 3 g

Pumpkin Pie

1   cup canned pumpkin

1/2   cup granulated sugar

1/2   cup packed brown sugar

1/2   teaspoon each cinnamon, ginger and salt

2   egg yolks

1/2   cup each heavy cream and milk

1   unbaked (8-inch) pie shell

   Ground nutmeg

Mix the first 9 ingredients in a bowl and. Pour into the pie shell. Sprinkle with nutmeg. Bake at 450 degrees for 10 minutes. Reduce the oven temperature to 325 degrees and bake for 30 to 45 minutes longer or until a knife inserted near the center comes out clean. Cool before slicing.

Makes 8 servings

Per serving

Calories 190 • Fat 7 g • Cholesterol 75 mg • Sodium 240 mg • Carbohydrate 30 g • Fiber 0 g • Protein 2 g

In 1910 Mable Skinner was elected Queen of the National Apple Show.

—Mesa County Colorado: A 100-Year History

Christmas Pie

PIE

6   all-purpose apples, peeled and sliced

1   cup fresh cranberries

1   cup chopped dates

1/4   teaspoon ground cinnamon

1/4   teaspoon ground cloves

3   tablespoons all-purpose flour

3/4   to 1 cup sugar

1/2   cup water

1/2   cup chopped walnuts
       Pastry Crust (below)

PASTRY CRUST

1   cup all-purpose flour

1/4   teaspoon salt

1/3   to 1/2 cup shortening

2   tablespoons cold water

For the pie, combine the apples, cranberries, dates, cinnamon and cloves in a large bowl. Add the flour and mix well. Combine the sugar and water in a large saucepan; bring to a boil. Reduce the heat and stir in the apple mixture. Cook for 10 minutes, stirring occasionally. Cool slightly. Stir in the walnuts. Spoon into the prepared crust, spreading evenly. Cool before slicing. Garnish with baked pastry cut into holiday shapes.

For the crust, combine the flour and salt in a small bowl. Cut in the shortening until crumbly. Add the water, 1 tablespoon at a time, mixing with a fork until the mixture forms a ball. Roll into a 10-inch circle on a lightly floured surface. Fit into a 9-inch pie plate. Flute the edge. Line the pastry shell with foil to cover; fill with pie weights or dried beans. Bake at 450 degrees for 12 to 15 minutes or until golden brown. Cool.

Makes 8 servings

Per serving

Calories 450 • Fat 17 g • Cholesterol 0 mg • Sodium 75 mg • Carbohydrate 73 g • Fiber 6 g • Protein 4 g

Double-Crust Peach Cobbler

PASTRY

5	cups all-purpose flour
1	teaspoon salt
1 1/4	cups extra-light olive oil
3/4	cup milk

FILLING

5	cups sliced, peeled Palisade peaches
1	cup granulated sugar or packed brown sugar
1 1/2	tablespoons cornstarch
1	teaspoon ground cinnamon
2	tablespoons butter, melted
	Additional sugar (optional)

For the pastry, combine the flour and salt in a large bowl. Add the olive oil and milk, stirring to form a ball. Divide the dough in half. Roll out each half between sheets of waxed paper to 12×18-inch rectangles. Fit 1 rectangle into a 9×13-inch baking dish.

For the filling, combine the peaches, 1 cup sugar, cornstarch, cinnamon and butter in a large bowl and mix well. Spoon into the pastry-lined baking dish. Top with the remaining pastry rectangle. Seal the edges of the dough and flute if desired. Cut slits in the top pastry. Sprinkle with additional sugar. Bake at 400 degrees for 25 to 30 minutes or until the topping is golden brown. Cool 10 minutes before serving. Serve warm.

Makes 12 servings

One of the first orchards was planted in 1883 along the Colorado River.

—Mesa County Colorado: A 100-Year History

Sponsored By

Carol Todd

Per serving
Calories 570 • Fat 27 g • Cholesterol 5 mg • Sodium 220 mg • Carbohydrate 77 g • Fiber 2 g • Protein 6 g

Rich Chocolate Tart

CHOCOLATE TART

1   cup plus 6 tablespoons heavy cream

2   tablespoons granulated sugar

    Pinch of salt

1   pound good-quality semisweet or bittersweet chocolate, chopped

1/2 cup (1 stick) unsalted butter, softened

1/2 cup milk

    Butter Crust (below)

    Confectioners' sugar for dusting

BUTTER CRUST

3/4 cup confectioners' sugar

1 1/2 cups all-purpose flour

    Dash of salt

9   tablespoons (1 stick plus 1 tablespoon) cold unsalted butter, cut up

2   egg yolks

2   tablespoons ice water

For the tart, combine the cream, sugar and salt in a large heavy saucepan; bring to a boil. Remove from the heat; whisk in the chocolate and butter until smooth. Stir in the milk. Remove the crust from the pan and place on a serving platter. Pour the filling into the crust. Chill for 1 hour or until set. Dust with confectioners' sugar. Garnish each serving with a dollop of sour cream. The tart may be made 1 day ahead and chilled. Let stand at room temperature for 2 hours.

For the crust, process the confectioners' sugar, flour and salt in a food processor. Add the butter and pulse until the mixture is crumbly. Whisk the egg yolks and water together in a small bowl; add to the flour mixture. Process until moistened. Form into a ball. Wrap in plastic wrap and chill for 1 hour or until firm. Roll out into a 14-inch circle on a lightly floured surface. Fit into a 12-inch tart pan with removable bottom. Freeze for 1 hour. Line the pastry shell with foil to cover; fill with pie weights or dried beans. Bake at 350 degrees for 15 minutes. Remove the foil and weights. Bake for 10 minutes longer or until golden brown. Cool in the pan on a wire rack.

Makes 12 servings

Per serving

Calories 320 • Fat 23 g • Cholesterol 80 mg • Sodium 25 mg • Carbohydrate 28 g • Fiber 9 g • Protein 3 g

Black Bottom Custard Squares

14 graham crackers, finely crushed
(about 1 cup)

5 tablespoons butter, melted

4 egg yolks

1/2 cup sugar

1 1/4 teaspoons cornstarch

2 cups milk

1 teaspoon vanilla extract

1 envelope unflavored gelatin

1/4 cup water

1 1/2 ounces bittersweet chocolate, melted
Dash of salt

1/2 cup sugar

1/4 teaspoon cream of tartar

4 egg whites, at room temperature

1 teaspoon vanilla extract

Combine the graham cracker crumbs and butter in a bowl and press onto the bottom of a 9×9-inch baking pan. Bake at 300 degrees for 10 minutes. Whisk the egg yolks in a bowl. Whisk in 1/2 cup sugar, the cornstarch and milk until well blended. Pour the mixture into the top of a double boiler or a heavy saucepan. Cook over hot water until thickened to a custard consistency (coats a spoon), stirring frequently. Stir in 1 teaspoon vanilla. Meanwhile, combine the gelatin and water; let stand for 5 minutes. Whisk together 1 cup of the hot custard with the melted chocolate and salt in a small bowl until well blended. Spread over the crust. Stir the softened gelatin into the remaining hot custard and mix well. Cool slightly. Combine 1/2 cup sugar and the cream of tartar. Beat the egg whites in a mixing bowl until moist peaks form. Beat in the sugar mixture and 1 teaspoon vanilla gradually until stiff peaks form. Fold into the custard. Spread over the chocolate layer. Refrigerate until firm. Garnish with chocolate curls. Note: You may substitute 1 tablespoon rum for the vanilla.

Makes 6 servings

Per serving

Calories 360 • Fat 15 g • Cholesterol 125 mg • Sodium 260 mg • Carbohydrate 48 g • Fiber 1 g • Protein 8 g

Lemon Curd Bars

CRUST

1 1/2 cups all-purpose flour

1/4 cup confectioners' sugar

3/4 cup (1 1/2 sticks) cold unsalted butter, chopped

LEMON FILLING

6 eggs

3 cups sugar

Grated zest of 1 lemon

1 cup plus 2 tablespoons fresh lemon juice (about 6 lemons)

1/2 cup all-purpose flour

For the crust, sift together the flour and confectioners' sugar into a large bowl. Add the butter and cut in with a pastry blender or 2 knives until crumbly. Press the mixture onto the bottom and 3/4 inch up the sides of a 9×13-inch baking pan. Bake at 325 degrees for 20 to 30 minutes or until golden brown. Set aside to cool slightly. Reduce the oven temperature to 300 degrees.

For the filling, whisk together the eggs and sugar in a large bowl until well blended. Stir in the lemon zest and lemon juice. Sift 1/2 cup flour over the lemon mixture and mix well. Pour over the crust. Bake for about 35 minutes or until set. Remove to a wire rack to cool completely before cutting into bars.

Makes 18 servings

Sponsored By

Gretchen Rose Aldrich

Per serving

Calories 285 • Fat 10 g • Cholesterol 90 mg • Sodium 25 mg • Carbohydrate 47 g • Fiber 1 g • Protein 3 g

Peaches & Cream Cheese Bars

3¹/₂ cups all-purpose flour

1¹/₂ cups sugar

1¹/₂ cups chopped pecans

1¹/₂ cups (3 sticks) butter, softened

1 egg

8 ounces cream cheese, softened

¹/₂ cup sugar

1 egg

1 teaspoon lemon juice

1 (16-ounce) jar peach jam

Combine the flour, 1¹/₂ cups sugar, pecans, butter and 1 egg in a large mixing bowl. Beat at low speed for 2 to 3 minutes or until the mixture is crumbly, scraping the side of the bowl frequently. Reserve 2 cups of the crumb mixture. Press the remaining crumb mixture onto the bottom of a greased 9×13-inch baking pan. Bake at 350 degrees for 10 minutes. Meanwhile, combine the cream cheese and ¹/₂ cup sugar in a mixing bowl; beat until well blended. Beat in 1 egg and the lemon juice until smooth and creamy. Remove the crust from the oven. Spread the cream cheese mixture evenly over the crust. Spoon the jam over the cream cheese layer, spreading evenly. Sprinkle with the reserved crumb mixture. Bake for 40 to 45 minutes or until lightly browned. Remove to a wire rack to cool completely before cutting into bars.

Makes 24 servings

Fairs were started to promote the region's produce. In 1885, ten thousand Peach Day visitors arrived on specials the railroad promoted.

—Mesa County Colorado: A 100-Year History

Per serving
Calories 380 • Fat 21 g • Cholesterol 60 mg • Sodium 120 mg • Carbohydrate 44 g • Fiber 1 g • Protein 4 g

Cowboy Cookies

1   cup (2 sticks) unsalted butter, softened

1   cup granulated sugar

1   cup packed brown sugar

2   eggs

1   teaspoon vanilla extract

2 1/2 cups all-purpose flour

1   teaspoon baking soda

1/2 teaspoon salt

2   cups rolled oats

1   cup semisweet chocolate chips

Cream the butter, granulated sugar and brown sugar in a large mixing bowl until light and fluffy. Add the eggs and vanilla and beat for 2 minutes. Stir together the flour, baking soda and salt. Add the flour mixture gradually to the butter mixture and mix well. Stir in the oats and chocolate chips. Drop by spoonfuls onto an ungreased cookie sheet. Bake at 350 degrees for 12 minutes. Immediately remove the cookies to a wire rack to cool. The cookies will be moist and chewy. Note: You may replace 1/2 cup of the oats with 1/2 cup wheat germ.

Makes 6 dozen

Sponsored By

Grand Valley National Bank

Per serving

Calories 80 • Fat 3.5 g • Cholesterol 15 mg • Sodium 40 mg • Carbohydrate 11 g • Fiber 0 g • Protein 1 g

Iced Ginger Cookies

COOKIES

¹/₂	cup (1 stick) butter, softened
1	cup sugar
1	egg
1	cup molasses
4	cups all-purpose flour
2	teaspoons ground ginger
1	teaspoon ground cinnamon
1	teaspoon ground cloves
1	teaspoon ground nutmeg
¹/₂	teaspoon salt
2	teaspoons baking soda
1	cup hot water
	Icing (below)

ICING

¹/₄	cup (¹/₂ stick) butter, softened
2	cups confectioners' sugar
1	teaspoon (or more) cream or orange juice

For the cookies, cream the butter and sugar in a large mixing bowl until light and fluffy. Beat in the egg and molasses until well blended. Stir together the flour, ginger, cinnamon, cloves, nutmeg and salt; add to the butter mixture and mix well. Stir the baking soda into the water until dissolved; add to the dough and mix well. Drop by spoonfuls onto a nonstick cookie sheet. Bake at 400 degrees for 8 minutes. Remove the cookies to a wire rack. Spread with the icing while warm.

For the icing, cream the butter and sugar in a mixing bowl until light and fluffy. Stir in the cream to the desired consistency.

Makes 6 dozen

Per serving

Calories 80 • Fat 2 g • Cholesterol 10 mg • Sodium 70 mg • Carbohydrate 14 g • Fiber 0 g • Protein 1 g

Sour Cream Sugar Cookies

4¹/2 cups all-purpose flour
1 teaspoon baking powder
1 teaspoon baking soda
1 teaspoon salt
1 cup (2 sticks) butter, softened
1¹/2 cups sugar
2 eggs
1 cup sour cream
1¹/2 teaspoons vanilla extract
1 (16-ounce) container vanilla frosting

Stir together the flour, baking powder, baking soda and salt and set aside. Cream the butter and sugar in a large mixing bowl until light and fluffy. Beat in the eggs until well blended. Add the flour mixture alternately with the sour cream and mix well. Stir in the vanilla. Divide the dough in half. Wrap each dough ball in plastic wrap and refrigerate for 2 hours. Cut each dough ball into quarters. Roll ¹/8 inch thick on a lightly floured surface. Cut with a cookie cutter or thin-rimmed glass. Place on an ungreased cookie sheet. Repeat with the remaining dough. Bake at 375 degrees for 10 to 12 minutes or until the bottoms of the cookies are golden brown. Cool on a wire rack. Spread with the frosting.

Makes 4 dozen

Per serving
Calories 155 • Fat 7 g • Cholesterol 20 mg • Sodium 135 mg • Carbohydrate 21 g • Fiber 0 g • Protein 2 g

Enstrom's Toffee Butter Cookies

3   cups all-purpose flour

1   teaspoon salt

1/2   teaspoon baking soda

1   cup (2 sticks) butter, softened

1   cup sugar

2   eggs

1   tablespoon vanilla extract

10   ounces Enstrom's Almond Toffee, crushed

Stir together the flour, salt and baking soda and set aside. Cream the butter and sugar in a large mixing bowl until light and fluffy. Beat in the eggs and vanilla until well blended. Add the flour mixture gradually and mix well. Stir in the toffee. Form the dough into several logs, 2 inches in diameter; wrap tightly in plastic wrap. Refrigerate until well chilled. Cut into 1/4-inch slices. Place 2 inches apart on a greased cookie sheet. Bake at 375 degrees for 8 to 10 minutes or until the edges are light brown (do not overbake). Cool on the cookie sheet for 2 minutes. Remove to a wire rack to cool completely. Store in an airtight container.

Makes 4 dozen

From

Enstrom's Candies

Per serving

Calories 110 • Fat 7 g • Cholesterol 20 mg • Sodium 105 mg • Carbohydrate 11 g • Fiber 0 g • Protein 1 g

White Chocolate Macadamia Nut Cookies

1   cup (2 sticks) butter, softened
1¹/2 cups packed brown sugar
2   eggs
2   teaspoons vanilla extract
3   cups all-purpose flour
1¹/2 teaspoons baking powder
1   teaspoon salt
2   cups white chocolate chips
     (about 11 ounces)
1   cup chopped macadamia nuts

Cream the butter and brown sugar in a large mixing bowl until light and fluffy. Beat in the eggs 1 at a time. Stir in the vanilla. Stir together the flour, baking powder and salt; add to the butter mixture and mix well. Stir in the chocolate chips and nuts. Refrigerate the dough for at least 2 hours. Drop by large spoonfuls onto a nonstick cookie sheet. Bake at 350 degrees for 12 to 15 minutes (the cookies will be soft but not brown). Cool on the cookie sheet for 20 minutes. Remove to a wire rack to cool completely.

Makes 3 dozen

Sponsored By

Blanchard Insurance Group, Inc.

Per serving
Calories 165 • Fat 8 g • Cholesterol 25 mg • Sodium 275 mg • Carbohydrate 22 g • Fiber 1 g • Protein 2 g

Cinnamon-Spiced Biscotti

1 cup granulated sugar

1 cup packed dark brown sugar

1/2 to 3/4 cup sliced almonds

1/3 cup vegetable oil

2 teaspoons ground cinnamon

1 teaspoon ground cloves

2 teaspoons water

2 egg whites

1 egg

2 1/2 cups all-purpose flour

2 teaspoons baking powder

Combine the granulated sugar, brown sugar, almonds, oil, cinnamon, cloves, water, egg whites and egg in a large mixing bowl. Beat at low speed for 1 minute. Stir together the flour and baking powder; add gradually to the sugar mixture, beating until well blended (the dough will be soft). Divide the dough into 3 mounds; spoon onto a large cookie sheet coated with nonstick cooking spray. Form each mound into a 3/4-inch-thick rectangle (about 4×6 inches). Separate the rectangles on the cookie sheet to allow for spreading during baking. Bake at 375 degrees for 25 minutes. Remove to a wire rack and cool for 10 minutes. Cut diagonally into 3/4-inch slices. Cool completely.

Makes 2 dozen

Per serving

Calories 160 • Fat 4.5 g • Cholesterol 10 mg • Sodium 45 mg • Carbohydrate 27 g • Fiber 1 g • Protein 2 g

Lemon and White Chocolate Biscotti

3/4 cup sugar

2 eggs

2 teaspoons grated lemon zest

1 teaspoon vanilla extract

1/4 teaspoon lemon extract

1 2/3 cups all-purpose flour

1/2 teaspoon baking soda

1/4 teaspoon salt

6 ounces premium white chocolate, chopped (or white chocolate chips)

Combine the sugar, eggs, lemon zest, vanilla extract and lemon extract in a large mixing bowl. Beat at medium speed until well blended. Stir together the flour, baking soda and salt; add gradually to the sugar mixture and mix well. Stir in the white chocolate. Divide the dough in half; turn onto a large cookie sheet coated with nonstick cooking spray. Form into 2 rolls (about 2 1/2 x 12 inches). Bake at 300 degrees for 35 minutes. Remove to a wire rack and cool for 10 minutes. Cut each roll diagonally into twenty-four 1/2-inch slices. Place the slices, cut side down, on the cookie sheet. Bake at 300 degrees for 10 to 12 minutes. Turn the cookies over; bake for 10 minutes longer (the cookies will be slightly soft in the center). Remove to a wire rack and cool completely.

Makes 4 dozen

Sponsored By

Keith and Kathleen Killian

Per serving

Calories 50 • Fat 1.5 g • Cholesterol 10 mg • Sodium 35 mg • Carbohydrate 9 g • Fiber 0 g • Protein 1 g

Barn Burner Coffee

1/4 cup packed brown sugar

1 teaspoon ground cinnamon

1 lime, cut in half

6 ounces (3/4 cup) Kahlúa or other coffee-flavored liqueur

4 ounces (1/2 cup) brandy

4 cups (or more) freshly brewed coffee
  Whipped cream

Combine the brown sugar and cinnamon in a small shallow dish. Rub the lime around the rims of 4 mugs or cups; dip the rims in the brown sugar mixture to coat. Add 1 1/2 ounces Kahlúa and 1 ounce brandy to each mug. Fill with coffee and top with whipped cream. Sprinkle with additional cinnamon if desired. Note: This is potent. Have a designated driver available!

Makes 4 servings

Per serving
Calories 270 • Fat <1 g • Cholesterol 0 mg • Sodium 15 mg • Carbohydrate 32 g • Fiber 0 g • Protein <1 g

Peach Brandy

2 cups brandy

1 cup sugar

1 cinnamon stick, broken

4 cups sliced peeled peaches

Combine the brandy, sugar, cinnamon stick and peaches in a large jar. Refrigerate, covered, for 4 to 6 weeks, shaking occasionally. Strain; discard the solids.

Makes 4 to 6

Per serving
Calories 517 • Fat .5 g • Cholesterol 0 mg • Sodium 1 mg • Carbohydrate 66 g • Fiber 3 g • Protein 2 g

Downhill skiing was first attempted on the southwest slope of Land's End Road in 1936-37.

—Mesa County Colorado: A 100-Year History

Huntin' Camp Bloody Mary

1/2 cup Bloody Mary mix (preferably Major Peter's)

2 tablespoons (1 ounce) vodka

1/2 teaspoon Creole seasoning

1/2 teaspoon lemon juice

1/2 teaspoon Worcestershire sauce

1/4 teaspoon Tabasco sauce, or to taste

1 cup (about) crushed ice

Celery rib

Combine the Bloody Mary mix, vodka, Creole seasoning, lemon juice, Worcestershire sauce and Tabasco sauce in a tall glass and mix well. Add the ice and celery.

Makes 1 serving

Per serving

Calories 87 • Fat <1 g • Cholesterol 0 mg • Sodium 1010 mg • Carbohydrate 5 g • Fiber 1 g • Protein 1 g

Watermelon Margaritas

1 cup watermelon chunks

1/2 cup tequila

1/2 cup Triple Sec

4 to 6 ounces frozen limeade concentrate

Ice

Combine the watermelon, tequila, Triple Sec and limeade concentrate in a blender. Add ice to fill the blender container; blend until the ice is crushed. Garnish each serving with a lime slice. Note: Other fresh fruit may be used instead of watermelon.

Makes 4 to 6 servings

Per serving

Calories 259 • Fat <1 g • Cholesterol 0 mg • Sodium 6 mg • Carbohydrate 36 g • Fiber <1 g • Protein <1 g

Raspberry Martini

1/2 ounce (1 tablespoon) raspberry liqueur
1 ounce (2 tablespoons) vodka
1 ounce (2 tablespoons) pineapple juice
Cracked ice

Combine all the ingredients in a cocktail shaker; shake well. Strain into a chilled cocktail glass and garnish with a lemon twist.

Makes 1 serving

Per serving
Calories 120 • Fat <1 g • Cholesterol 0 mg • Sodium 1 mg • Carbohydrate 9 g • Fiber <1 g • Protein <1 g

Roasted Lemon Martini

MARTINI
1 lemon, roasted (see Note)
1 ounce (2 tablespoons) Simple Syrup (below)
2 ounces (1/4 cup) vodka
Crushed ice

For the martini, cut off both ends of the roasted lemon; cut into 4 thick slices. Combine the lemon slices, syrup and vodka with the ice in a cocktail shaker; shake well. Strain into a chilled martini glass. Note: To roast lemons, wash and dry the lemons. Place on a baking sheet (on a layer of coarse salt if desired). Bake at 325 degrees for 1 hour, turning once. Cool completely.

SIMPLE SYRUP
1 cup sugar
1/2 cup water

For the syrup, bring the sugar and water to a boil in a small saucepan. Cook just until the sugar is dissolved, stirring frequently. Remove from the heat; cool.

Makes 1 serving

Per serving
Calories 255 • Fat 0 g • Cholesterol 0 mg • Sodium 6 mg • Carbohydrate 33 g • Fiber 1 g • Protein 0 g

Perked Cider

2 quarts apple cider
1/2 cup packed brown sugar
1 cinnamon stick, broken
1 teaspoon whole cloves
1/2 teaspoon whole allspice
Dash of ground nutmeg
1 orange (unpeeled), cut into wedges

Pour the cider into an 18-cup or larger coffee percolator. Place the brown sugar, cinnamon stick, cloves, allspice, nutmeg and orange wedges in the percolator basket. Perk until the cider is hot.

Makes 8 servings

The city library was built in 1901 on the corner of 7th and Grand. Andrew Carnegie was appealed with a large sum of money for the building.

—Mesa County Colorado:
A 100-Year History

Sponsored By

Karen, Mike, and Mikey Anton

Per serving
Calories 170 • Fat 0 g • Cholesterol 0 mg • Sodium 30 mg • Carbohydrate 43 g • Fiber 0 g • Protein 0 g

Peach Sangria

2   ripe peaches, peeled and thinly sliced
1/2   cup peach schnapps
1/3   cup sugar
3   cups rosé, chilled
2   cups sparkling water, chilled

Combine the peaches, schnapps and sugar in a large pitcher and mix well. Let stand for at least 1 hour. Stir in the wine and sparkling water. Serve over ice if desired.

Makes 8 servings

Per serving
Calories 137 • Fat <1 g • Cholesterol 0 mg • Sodium 5 mg • Carbohydrate 12 g • Fiber <1 g • Protein <1 g

Sangria

1   (12-ounce) can frozen fruit
      punch concentrate, thawed
2   cups water
1   cup white wine or rosé, chilled
      Ice
      Orange, lemon or lime slices

Combine the concentrate, water and wine in a large pitcher, stirring until well blended. Add ice and orange slices. Serve chilled.

Makes 8 servings

Colorado Mountain Vineyards, on East Orchard Mesa, began local wine production from Grand Valley grapes in 1980.

—Mesa County Colorado: A 100-Year History

Per serving
Calories 105 • Fat <1 g • Cholesterol 0 mg • Sodium 6 mg • Carbohydrate 22 g • Fiber <1 g • Protein <1 g

Credits

DAVE FISHELL
Museum of Western Colorado

A LAND ALONE: COLORADO'S WESTERN SLOPE
By Duane Vandenbusche and Duane A. Smith

A SPIRIT OF CHARITY
St. Mary's Hospital Celebrating a Century of Caring
By Dave Fishell

MESA COUNTY COLORADO: A 100-YEAR HISTORY
Museum of Western Colorado Press
By Emma McCreznor

THE GRAND HERITAGE: A PHOTOGRAPHIC HISTORY OF GRAND JUNCTION, COLORADO
By Dave Fishell

HISTORICAL ATLAS OF COLORADO
By Thomas J. Noel, Paul F. Mahoney, Richard E. Stevens

PHOTOGRAPHERS
Christopher Tomlinson
734 South Seventh Street
Grand Junction, Colorado 81501

Randy Price

Cookbook Committee

CO-CHAIRS
Kathleen Copeland
Joan Graham

RECIPE COLLECTION AND CODING
Gretchen Sodamann

GRAPHICS AND LAYOUT
Traeana Tripoli

NUTRITIONAL ANALYSIS
Pat Stiles

MARKETING
Amy Lusby

NON-RECIPE TEXT
Karen Anton
Doris Walck

PROMOTIONS
Cyn Watts
Amy Milyard

PUBLIC RELATIONS
Ann Nichols
Pam Francil

STEERING COMMITTEE
Terri Schmitt
Ashley Elliott
Rebecca Rolland
Marcee Walck
Jodie Brandon
Patti Milius
Krista Gibson
Holly Garcia
Dottie Craven
Kim Jones
Tina Marie Mahlum

PHOTOGRAPHY
Christopher Tomlinson
Randy Price

PROOFREADING
Dave Haynes

Special thanks go to William and Patti Milius for the office space and to all the members of Junior Service League for their help and support, especially for those who submitted the wonderful recipes and who held tasting parties. Thanks go to Dixie Burmeister for her encouragement and for writing the foreword for *Celebrate Colorado*. Dave Fishell and other local authors deserve a big thank-you for providing us with so much history and interesting information about this beautiful area in which we live. We also want to give special thanks to Jeff Copeland and Tom Graham, who have helped out in so many ways with this endeavor.

Contributors

Jackie Aguilar
Louise Antrim
Marcee Applegate
Dawn Arnett
Mandi Aubert
Ruth Barnes
Barb Baxter
Patricia Belcastro
Bennett's Restaurant
Pat Bishop
Blue Moon Bar & Grille
Jane Bohall
Jody Brandon
Becky Bridges
Ryan Brown
Susan Brown
Emily Buchanan
Barbara Chamberlin
Bernetta Charlesworth
Ruth Coatney
Margaret Coe
Tony Colaizzi
Anne Connolly
Kathleen Copeland
John D. Cornett
Mary Cornforth-Cawood
Lynn Cotton
Dottie Craven
Mindi Daniel
Debra Docter
Grayce Dvirnak
Enstrom's Candies
Joanna Feather
Amanda Fernstein
Ruth Ann Field

Suzette Fletcher
Jan Francis
Tracey Garchar
Lorraine M. Garcia
Amy Gibbs
Joan Graham
Julie Graham
Diane Griffiths
Tonja Guccini
Ann Guth
Joyce Hackbert
Dave Haynes
Tanya Hester
Cheryl Hill
Janet Hollingsworth
Alberta Hush
Il Bistro Italiano Restaurant
Helen James
Judy Jeter
Marty Jones
George Jouflas
Judi Kugeler
Dorothy LaCount
Patsy Lahue
Kathy Leech
Tina Marie Mahlum
Main Street Cafe
Janice Matticks
Nancy McBride
Zelma McDonald
Heather Meyers
Patti Milius
Toni Milyard
Janet Moore-Cox
Jessica Morganstein

Dorothy Morrison
Nero's Restaurant
Brenda Nesbitt
Charlene Newton
Anne Nichols
William O'Brien
Pablos Pizza
Leonard Polzine
Synthia Polzine
Linda Quarles
Lynette Rajala
Carol Rasmussen
Gretchen Richardson
Bonny Rininger
Karen Roberts
Rockslide Brewery
Illene Roggensack
Elaine Rydiger
Glenda Scheuerman
Sue Schmitt
Terri Schmitt
Sue Setje
Jamee Simons
Shirley Skinner
Marianne Smith
Gretchen Sodamann
Pat Stiles
Shirley Teets
Diane Thompson
Christopher Tomlinson
Tubac Deli
Sheryl VanHole
Mary Verdieck
Marilyn S. Veselack
Vineyard Wine & Fine Dining, The

Doris Walck
Nancy Walter
Karel Watson
Cyn Watts
Connie Whalen
Robyn Willie
Frances Williamson
Laurie Williamson
Sherry Williamson
Wendy Williamson
Meryll Woodcock
Julie Zancanelli

Testers

Gretchen Aldrich
Arlene Baker
Cheri Barkhe
Jody Brandon
Lynn Brangdon
Janet Brink
Shirley Burcholder
Alena Busovska
Julie Butherus
Barbara and Ed Chamberlain
Anne Connolly
Kathleen Copeland
Jeff Copeland
Lynn Cotton
Dottie Craven
Ashley Elliott
Lori Emerson
Marissa Felix
Carolyn Ford

Jan Francis
Krista Gibson
Joan Graham
Janet Hollingsworth
Judi Kuegler
Tonja Kueper
Michael Kuzminski
Stephanie Lucas
Anne Lucnoli
Andy Martsolf
Janelle Meyer
Patti Milius
Amy Milyard
Tyler Milyard
Charlotte Nardi
Anne Nichols
Judy Panozzo
JoAnne Pearson
Synthia Polzine
Rebecca Rike
Karen Roberts
Terri Schmitt
Gretchen Sodamann
Pat Stiles
Traeana Tripoli
Joe Tripoli
Sheryl VanHole
Doris Walck
Karel Watson
Cyn Watts

Index

Junior Service League of Grand Junction

P.O. Box 2385 • Grand Junction, CO 81502
Phone/Fax: (970) 243-7790
www.jslgj.com

Thank you for your order! Proceeds from the sale of these cookbooks support the purpose and the programs of The Junior Service League of Grand Junction, Incorporated.

Order Date: _____

Name _____

Street Address _____

City _____ State _____ Zip Code _____

Telephone _____

(If you are shipping to a different address, please indicate this and write the shipping address on the back of this order form.)

Number of Books Ordered:

West of the Rockies _____ @ $17.95 per book $ _____
Recipes from Campfire to Candlelight

Celebrate Colorado _____ @ $27.95 per book $ _____
West of the Rockies

Subtotal $ _____

*Shipping/Handling $ _____

**Tax $ _____

Grand Total $ _____

***Shipping/Handling:** $4.95 for first book; $2.00 for each additional book going to the same address

****Tax:** 2.9% if Colorado shipping address; 7.65% if city of Grand Junction shipping address

Method of Payment: [　] MasterCard   [　] VISA
[　] Check enclosed payable to Junior Service League

Credit Card Number _____ Expiration Date _____

Signature _____ (or) Check Number _____

Prices are subject to change without notice.

Photocopies will be accepted.